"Sherrie Campbell has created another wonderful gem of a book for survivors of emotionally abusive parents. She has thoughtfully created a labor of love through her own wisdom, knowledge, experience, and research. This book is like a bible for survivors who didn't have words to describe what they were going through, felt unlovable, or felt misunderstood when discussing their experiences of emotional abuse."

—**Natalie Jones, PsyD, LPCC**, expert therapist in narcissistic abuse, wellness consultant, corporate consultant, speaker, and expert witness

"*Adult Survivors of Emotionally Abusive Parents* takes a deep, relatable, and honest look into the traumas caused by emotionally abusive parents. Sherrie Campbell unpacks the insidiousness of emotional abuse—why and how it's hard to prove, and how challenging it can be for survivors to live with the aftereffects. This book is an inspirational, healing guide that teaches each survivor how to be their own superhero."

—**Ande Anderson, MS, RD**, co-owner of AVAIYA

"I encourage any adult who has experienced emotional abuse at the hands of a parent or caregiver, regardless of the background, to seek the truth through Sherrie Campbell's words. My full endorsement of *Adult Survivors of Emotionally Abusive Parents* can be given with confidence not only because I've lived it, but Campbell's compassion and expertise have been sources of peace and improvement in my life."

—**Kevin P. Donaldson**, retired police officer, survivor of emotionally abusive parents, and author

"If you were raised by an emotionally abusive parent, this book is your road map to recovery. Sherrie Campbell captures the devastating impact of toxic parenting and takes you on a journey that not only helps you understand what happened, but also gives you strategies to thrive. She also weaves her own personal journey throughout, serving as an inspiration and reminder that you are not alone, and recovery is possible."

—**Krylyn Peters, LPC**, psychotherapist, educator, and consultant

"With her trademark honesty, compassion, and insight, Sherrie Campbell reveals the features of emotionally abusive parents, and busts the societal myths that allow such behaviors to continue unchallenged. She comes alongside the reader as someone who has been there, helping them understand their feelings while providing a comprehensive toolbox of strategies to recover from the devastating symptoms of parental abuse—so they can have the authentic, fulfilling life they deserve."

—**Laura K. Connell**, trauma-informed coach and author of *It's Not Your Fault*

T0000793

"How does one overcome the trauma, guilt, and pain from growing up with emotionally abusive parents? Sherrie Campbell offers applicable strategies toward a path of healing in her new book, *Adult Survivors of Emotionally Abusive Parents*. Campbell's zone of genius shines in an area that doesn't get enough exposure. Being a survivor herself, Campbell guides readers with a genuine understanding of the path to self-love and emotional freedom."

> —**Shawn Marshall**, emotional intelligence/personal leadership expert

"Sherrie Campbell's work on toxic family dynamics is some of the most important work we can do as a human family. For far too long, we have been smothered under the blanket of toxic sayings like, 'Family is family.' Abuse is abuse. Campbell gives survivors not only a voice, but also the power to stop generational trauma in its path."

> —**Alison Canavan**, change agent, author, keynote speaker, and meditation teacher

"*Adult Survivors of Emotionally Abusive Parents* is an eye-opening exploration of the profound impact that emotionally abusive parents can have on our lives. A must-read for anyone seeking to understand, cope with, and ultimately heal from the challenges posed by the emotionally abusive parental dynamic. A powerful resource that sheds light on a transformative journey toward breaking toxic familial chains and healthy emotional liberation."

> —**Dave Arnold**, transformative coach on moving past narcissistic/ toxic relationships

"Sherrie Campbell's book serves as an indispensable contribution to family systems literature, drawing from her own survival experience as a family scapegoat. With courage and compassion, she shines a light on the emotional injuries endured by children who find themselves entangled in family toxicity. This book is a heartfelt invitation for healing and transformative change."

> —**Elena Herdieckerhoff**, intuitive life coach, business mentor, TEDx speaker, and CEO of Red Dot Stage

"Sherrie Campbell continues to go above and beyond to help survivors of emotionally abusive parents. This book, along with her other smash hits, helps ease the pain of childhood trauma while also giving applicable strategies to live your best life forward. Campbell has an incredible ability to help the reader feel comfortable in an uncomfortable situation by meeting the reader where they are at in their healing journey."

> —**DJ Hiller**, mental performance coach, and host of the *Mindset Advantage* podcast

Adult Survivors *of* Emotionally Abusive Parents

**How to Heal,
Cultivate Emotional Resilience &
Build the Life & Love You Deserve**

Sherrie Campbell, PhD

New Harbinger Publications, Inc.

Publisher's Note

This publication is designed to provide accurate and authoritative information in regard to the subject matter covered. It is sold with the understanding that the publisher is not engaged in rendering psychological, financial, legal, or other professional services. If expert assistance or counseling is needed, the services of a competent professional should be sought.

Distributed in Canada by Raincoast Books

NEW HARBINGER PUBLICATIONS is a registered trademark of New Harbinger Publications, Inc.

Copyright © 2024 by Sherrie Campbell
        New Harbinger Publications, Inc.
        5720 Shattuck Avenue
        Oakland, CA 94609
        www.newharbinger.com

Cover design by Amy Daniel

Acquired by Elizabeth Hollis Hansen

Edited by Elizabeth Dougherty

All Rights Reserved

Library of Congress Cataloging-in-Publication Data on file

FSC
www.fsc.org
MIX
Paper | Supporting
responsible forestry
FSC® C008955

Printed in the United States of America

26   25   24

10   9   8   7   6   5   4   3   2   1   First Printing

For my daughter, London

"There can be no keener revelation of a society's soul than the way in which it treats its children."

—Nelson Mandela

Contents

Moments of Truth

Not all parents are good parents.

Children have no option to choose their parents.

All children want to be good.

All children are susceptible to their parents' influence, positive or negative.

These truths cut to the core.

The myth that all parents are good is strongly perpetuated socially, religiously, and culturally, as well as in family law and, ironically, in the field of psychology and mental health. A hard truth to acknowledge is that not all parents are good parents. For example, some parents are severely character disordered, which means that they have a severe personality disorder. These parents may insist they love their children, but because these parents are unhealthy it would follow that whatever they believe about love is unhealthy. A dysfunctional parent's twisted idea of love is to force their own needs onto their children and expect automatic compliance. What these parents fail to grasp is that neither love nor connection can be forced. For this reason, it is critical to acknowledge the common misassumption that any time a child displays abnormal behaviors that the child is somehow the problem. Instead, the way in which parents treat their children and any accompanying trauma should be examined as the core source of those behaviors.

Children are born vulnerable and dependent. They are unable to support themselves physically, emotionally, mentally, relationally, financially, or spiritually well into their young adult years. Even then, most healthy parents support their children to some degree throughout their life. As their children age, healthy parents step back in developmentally appropriate increments, allowing their maturing children the space to meet their own needs. Healthy parents act as sources of assistance when their children seek it. Egocentric parents—that is, parents who are self-centered and self-absorbed—on the other hand, do not view parenting with the same vision as healthy parents. Toxic parents provide a mixed cocktail of making their children feel like they cannot get rid of them soon enough, in tandem with clutching to their children as tightly as possible the more their children naturally start separating from them. There is no way to function in a healthy way in the confusion of this "come close, go away" dynamic. In this dynamic, children feel uncertain as to when they are allowed to get their primary needs met and when they are not supposed to ask for or need anything at all.

> **Moment of truth:** When parents are too self-absorbed to meet the most basic need for love in a consistent and unconditional manner, children suffer.

I was and am such a child, and likely so are you. I have two deeply toxic parents. Each of them manipulated and mistreated me in their own way, leaving me feeling bereft, insecure, abandoned, repulsive, fundamentally unlovable, and unimportant. Yet, to my bewilderment, they each expected accessibility to me whenever it suited their needs. I was left in a perpetual state of confusion. I was made to feel like an annoyance that was largely in the way of their freedom yet was expected to be available at their beck and call. My needs never factored into the relationship between myself and my parents. My life was built around the meeting of their needs. I was the child who was shoved to the side as often as possible. I spent much of my childhood feeling alone and having nowhere to turn for support. I felt persistently sad and scared to death of life and people. I am not alone in this.

Since I started writing books about toxic family relationships, I have developed an incredible following of bravehearted people, like yourself, who have also cut off or drastically distanced themselves from the parents who raised them. As I discussed in my previous book, *Adult Survivors of Toxic Family Members* (Campbell 2022), there is a powerful cultural kickback toward those of us who have been forced to make this decision. Because of this negative kickback, estrangement from family, especially parents, continues as a silent epidemic very few openly talk about. Why? Because those who have not had this experience cannot imagine the depths of pain children of emotionally abusive parents experience. Outsiders stand in fierce opposition toward an abusive dynamic they cannot fathom truly exists.

The mindset of emotionally abusive and manipulative parents is juvenile. These parents erroneously believe that because they chose to bring you into the world or adopt you, that this gives them the freedom to mistreat you in whatever ways they choose, viewing you as obligated to tolerate it. The mindset they hold is: "I brought you into the world, therefore I can treat you however I want. You are not allowed to disagree because you're the child, and I will exploit your inherent need for me to make you feel like you owe me for the life I gave you." Emotionally abusive parents do not view parenting as a love relationship, but rather as a transactional relationship of ownership. To take advantage of the basic needs of a child is nothing short of grotesque. This distorted mindset is deeply dehumanizing. Children do not owe parents their life simply because they raised them. Children do not choose their parents or the ways their parents treat them. Because having a child is a parent's choice, it would make sense that the more responsible, skilled, and mature parent would see themselves as owing it to their less skilled, more vulnerable child to be purposeful in treating their child with the upmost love, nurturance, and respect.

Moment of truth: Children should not have to earn love. They should be able to rest in it.

Parents give you either a life to love or a life to hate because they are the source and director of your life from the moment you are born. When raised by deeply character disordered parents, you live a life under parents who bring you misery. Sadly, the more fearful and defeated you become, the more control your parent can assert over you. Egocentric parents make life feel like one long never-ending battle against the odds. No child deserves to be treated in this manner. This includes you.

The psychological damage accomplished by emotionally abusive parents to the self-worth of their children is inexplicable and often impossible for survivors of toxic parents to put into words. In these scenarios, it is often best to find a community of other survivors and experts who have also experienced parental mistreatment and abuse. In me, you have both. I have survived much trauma coming from two highly dysfunctional parents, and I have written about my journey from both a clinical and an experiential space to give you a path to follow and situations to relate to.

This book is another step up the mountain of your healing. You will be hearing many truths about toxic parents that I believe will be reflected in your own experience. (Please note that I am writing about what I have found to be the most common and frequently shared experiences of survivors of emotionally abusive parents. However, your unique experience may differ.)

This book will provide practical tools to keep you focused on your healing. These tools will assist and inspire you to live the life you have always deserved to live.

You are not alone.

Moment of truth: It is time we stop associating strength with the ability to smile through the tears and suffer in silence.

CHAPTER 1

The Critical Importance
of Parents

From the moment you are born, the first people you give your heart to are your parents, not by your choice, but due to their choice to bring you into their world. You give your love to them because they are all you have. The love from child to parent (initially) is unaltered, effortless, natural, pure, and necessary for survival. This love doesn't require anything to be earned because it is fundamental to the innocence of a child's heart and their inherent vulnerability. Now, imagine if the first people you gave your heart to were cruel, neglectful, and selfish, and exploited the purity of your love. What would happen then? Your innocence would be destroyed, and your love would be replaced with fear.

Nothing in the outside world has a more profound impact over who you are than the parents who raise you. The relationship you have with your parents establishes the way you think and feel about yourself. This relationship is influential enough to establish the foundation for your personality, life choices, and idea of your overall value throughout the course of your life. The relationship shared between parent and child has the most potent impact on your emotional resiliency as it pertains to the critical areas of your social, mental, and emotional health. The relationship with your parents should have been the most treasured and special bond for you and your parents to enjoy and nurture over the course of your lifetime.

Characteristics of Healthy Parents

We will begin our discussion by examining the difference between healthy and toxic parenting.

Healthy parenting starts before you are born. Healthy parents:

- see themselves as your visionaries

- are acutely aware of the enormous reliability and accountability that come along with their role as your parent

- understand that their parenting practices and your development are deeply symbiotic; therefore, it is their greatest desire to keep you safe, aware, and feeling loved

- are emotionally available

- meet your basic needs

- model healthy values

- are protective

- advocate for you

- grant you the necessary space to develop

- are committed to their own personal growth

- choose their words wisely

- are unselfish

Under the direction of healthy parents, family is a happy, clear, fun, expressive, understandable, predictable, and peaceful experience. For example:

- Emotions are talked through.

- Your questions are given responses.

- You are taught the necessary life skills.

- You are included in family decisions.

- Honest and accurate information is valued.

- Your interests are honored and supported.

- You are free to express love and affection.

- Issues around conflict are addressed directly and openly.

This is not the case when your parents are emotionally abusive. Toxic parents have children to feel power. Healthy parents have children to empower.

Moment of truth: A child who has never lacked a balanced upbringing will continue to advance for the rest of their lives.

Characteristics of Abusive Parents

Emotionally abusive parents are vastly different in their approach to parenting. It's common for these parents to announce to the world, "I would die for my children." This may sound valiant, but with toxic parents, these grandiose words prove not to be an accurate statement of reality. Healthy parents do not parent from a bold, dramatic sentiment that does not line up with the reality of how they treat their children. Instead of claiming they would die for their children, healthy parents make the conscious choice to live for their children. Psychologically abusive parents:

- Are transactional, not relational. You are a "thing" that must adhere to inflexible rules. Fairness is not a consideration.

- Prefer weekly reports rather than connection or rapport. Your value is measured based on performance rather than from a shared, engaging journey of life with you.

- Run a balance sheet of give-and-take, keeping financial and emotional ledgers to use against you to secure compliance.

- Nothing is given for free. Everything given is at risk of being taken away.

- Feel slighted when things don't go their way. You must do all you can to ensure your parents are happy and satisfied, even when the standards keep shifting.

- Seek to control rather than to connect.

- Make the rules and punish you if you don't follow them precisely, even when they're unclear.

- Believe children are responsible for their parents' happiness. You are not to complicate their life with your own needs for happiness.

- View children as having zero rights in the relationship.

Children understand they are not supposed to feel dread toward their parents, who are supposed to treasure them above all others. When you grow up feeling this kind of dread, it gives you the sense that you are different from others, causing you to feel bad about yourself for feeling so negative toward the people you call your parents. The last thing you're likely to consider when trying to understand the dislike you have for them is that your parents could be the direct cause of those feelings. This type of self-incrimination often renders you defenseless to express what you feel in words that others would be able to understand. This is how dysfunctional parents silence you from exposing their degrading treatment.

From this vantage point, it is easier to understand why so many adults in the United States are estranged from their parents and so many teenagers and young adults report abuse at the hands of their parents. These parents, all the while, deny any abuse, purporting that their children over-exaggerate and are dramatic and far too sensitive.

> **Moment of truth:** Parents give you either a life to love or a life to hate.

Emotionally Abusive Parents Deny Your Experience of Abuse

A theme common to emotionally abusive parents is the denial of their children's feelings and experiences. These parents claim to love their children. Maybe in their minds they do. They feign "wanting to know your reasons" for any given issue. However, couched under that statement is the reality that they see themselves as the judge and jury of all you need and desire to say and have already ruled against you. Their idea of parenting is placing you into forced servitude. When you express needs of your own, you receive a disgusted, retaliatory response. When your experience of their emotional abuse is deflected, dismissed, and/or denied, it robs you of your existence. When you are robbed of your voice, a long list of unwanted outcomes arises. Egocentric parents make you feel humiliated and inferior. When you do give voice to your pain, you are accused of "throwing your parents under the bus." These types of dismissals allow your emotionally abusive parents to hide in plain sight.

> **Moment of truth:** Healing is not possible when your reality is not given the proper outlet for validation.

Reality Doesn't Matter to Emotionally Abusive Parents

The type of narcissism common to emotionally abusive parents is not rooted in insecurity or an inability to process emotions, as much as the literature may state. Toxic parents function from entitlement and dishonesty, placing them at odds with reality. If, or when, you take the side of reality, you become their enemy. These types of parents are pathological liars who lie about the ways in which they abuse you to protect their pride. They find great joy in flying under the radar, getting away with their abuse.

Abuse is a conscious, intentional choice. No one and nothing unconscious forces any parent to grossly mistreat their children. Your parents know right from wrong and disregard that knowledge in favor of doing what they want. There are always other choices, and these choices are common knowledge to all human beings, learned from preschool forward. Too many people use the excuse that your parents are the way they are because they were wounded as children. Bottom line is your parents have wounded you, and you're not abusing your children or other people one after another. There is no excuse for abuse. Repeated mistakes made by highly dysfunctional parents aren't accidents, but a reflection of their poor character.

For example, a girl had a bank account opened for her at the age of fifteen with her mother as a cosigner, so she could start learning to manage money. This girl shared the angry text thread shared between herself and her mother, where this girl had confronted her mother for what her mother called "accidentally" taking out close to $15,000 from her account over the past two years. The girl pleaded with her mother to stop taking money from her account on numerous occasions. Her mother's response was to deny reality by saying, "Don't talk down to me. Accidents happen." Her mother's response was juvenile, at best. The mother shifted blame onto her daughter, making her daughter the bad guy. Because this mother paid her daughter back whenever caught, this mother believed all was well, that she had made up for her "carelessness." What this mother refused to look at was how deeply betrayed her daughter felt and how these financial dishonesties drove an intense emotional distance between them. Because this mother could not responsibly or mindfully manage monies spent or validate this girl's grievances, this girl closed that joint account and opened a new account her mother could not access.

No parent should access their child's personal money without permission. If a child did this same thing to a parent's bank account, there would be massive consequences.

Moment of truth: Toxic parents don't feel they need to ask children for permission because they feel entitled to forgiveness.

Not All Parents Are Good

From the youngest of ages, children are indoctrinated into the idea that all parents are good. If you google the word "parents," you will be flooded with images of picture-perfect, happy families. Flashes of tender smiles as parents watch their babies drift to sleep. Cozy autumn walks with a small child holding the reassuring hands of their parents. Siblings making cookie dough with both parents laughing—faces covered in flour. These pictures are truly heartwarming. You could spend hours scrolling through these glossy stock photos without finding a single photo of a child shedding tears that aren't being compassionately wiped away by their parent. We see these same images of perfect parents and happy homes on the covers of our magazines, in television commercials, and in our most culturally iconic sitcoms. But how would you feel if none of these images told your personal story? Children raised under abusive and manipulative parents know this cultural narrative is a fallacy yet have no way to give voice to this in a way that could penetrate the depth of this socially ingrained bias. In our society, it is considered amoral to threaten this false monolithic model of perfect parents and happy homes. This is why we rarely see opposing narratives that counter this myth in culturally open space. Until this myth can be debunked, many children and adult survivors of toxic parents continue to suffer from its effects.

As a culture, we lean in to protect parents, sacrificing our children. Children under dysfunctional parents are kept as prisoners to their parents' needs. The only option for these children is the loss of their freedom and the rights to author their own life story. Children of emotionally abusive parents must follow along in the false narrative, being mindful not to

11

tarnish their parents' image, because doing so could put their own survival at risk. They know not to be "too difficult" or express "negative feelings."

Children are sacrificed because they are the easiest to sweep under the rug. Children have no means or capacity to stand stronger than their authority figures, giving parents a free pass when it comes to mistreating their children. Bad parents are allowed to hide in plain sight. For example, when a parent harms their children, others jump in to perpetuate the myth that all parents are good and justify the mistreatment by saying, "Your parent means well." However, if it were a stranger abusing or being cruel to a child, that abusive behavior would never be tolerated, let alone given a free pass. Not only does this lack logic, but it also whitewashes the parent of any wrongdoing or having to take accountability for how poorly they treat their children. Instead, children are left with no other choice but to rationalize insanity to survive.

The label of "parent" doesn't rid an abusive person of their dysfunction and magically change them into someone loving and altruistic. If anything, being given the parent label gives an already abusive person a new arena in which to act out their abuses, couch it as parenting, and get away with it. Society fails to consider that all people, meaning all parents, consciously choose how they show up in relationships and treat people. It is fundamentally wrong to give people who become parents an invisible suit of goodness that erases their troubled personality, while the real victim is the voiceless child. Children need homes, not emotional prisons.

CHAPTER 2

The Search for Any Feeling of Home

From the moment the spark of life that was you entered this world, you looked for family. Some children were fortunate enough to have been born into or adopted by loving, healthy, high-functioning families. Those of you who were less fortunate have spent your life searching for that fundamental thing that has always been missing—loving parents. First, you searched for love from the parents who raised you. When there was no love to be found, most of you didn't give up on your search because you couldn't. The need for love and belonging is fundamental to survival. So, you kept trying to change yourself to become someone your parents could love. You kept searching the same empty, emotionally unavailable parents for a love and belonging that they would not provide, no matter how much love and effort you gave. You loved them anyway. You had to. Those were the rules.

Emotional Debt Paradigm

Emotionally abusive parents parent from subtraction rather than addition. They made sure everything you loved, desired, thought, felt, or said could be taken away and/or used against you. This included your possessions, time, power of choice, and voice—and parental love and support. Taking things away (creating an emotional debt) was the easiest way to take advantage of your vulnerability and gain your compliance. Your emotionally abusive parents may have given you time, money, and extravagant gifts, or even sent you to expensive schools, but it could all be used against you because your parents had the power to remove it.

With subtraction, you were left with emotional debt. Emotional debt is a mixed toxic cocktail of fear, uncertainty, instability, frustration, worry, and resentment that systematically builds up inside of you. Your emotionally abusive parents made you feel that you owed it to them to repay sacrifices you never asked them to make. These harsh statements implied that what your parents sacrificed for you robbed something essential from them that they would like to do or have for themselves. To fix the losses your parents supposedly incurred because of you, you offered to accept less, be less, do less, and say less, so they could do, be, or have more of what they wanted. The hope behind your offer was to make yourself less difficult and easier for your parents to love. When you offered to take less, this likely offended your parents. It was too strong a mirror into their selfishness. To shift the blame, they dosed you with statements of their love and devotion, which made no sense when how they treated you did not feel anything like love or devotion, just subtraction.

Selfish parents weaponize sacrifice and devotion. You were led to believe that your natural need for your parents' time, love, and attention was asking for too much. Their irritation manifested as a withdrawal of all of the things you needed to feel closer to them. This callous withdrawal created panic. Panic weakened your inner strength, making you even easier for them to take advantage of.

Moment of truth: Blatantly dismissing or harshly criticizing children doesn't produce better behavior in them.

Emotionally abusive parents do not make use of the concept of addition in their parenting. They do not add a consistent stream of joy, redirection, motivation, guidance, positive rewards, pep talks, celebrations, and emotional protection, let alone unconditional love. The best you will get from a toxic parent is conditional kindness.

Conditional Kindness

Emotionally abusive parents are aware that abuse doesn't work without intermittent doses of kindness. Your parents used intermittent doses of kindness (small moments of addition) to gain something from you that they needed for themselves in that moment. These random doses of affection often came out of nowhere, making their impact on you more intense than it should have been—which made the following rapid withdrawal of their kindness even more excruciating. These small rations of kindness increased the intensity of your cravings for the consistency and predictability of it. Living in the randomness of this swinging pendulum of love and abuse left you feeling undeserving of even the smallest morsels of their love.

Whatever tactics of love withdrawal your parents used, this "come here, go away" approach left me and many of you feeling intensely abandoned and painfully lonely. When I would show sadness at the withdrawal, I was snidely told that they gave everything up for me, so the fact that I would want more made me ungrateful and "I had better think about that." I believed them. I had always wished I could have been different than I was, a child they could like, because I so desperately wanted to feel a part of something. I, like you, wanted to have a meaningful and significant, not just dutiful, place in the hearts of my parents. When your parents are highly dysfunctional, the simplicities that should be natural to the parent-child relationship are absent. To soothe this pain, many of you, knowingly or unknowingly, resorted to creating a fantasy of family that fit in with the cultural ideal of perfect parents and happy homes as a path to your daily survival.

Creating Fantasy Parents

When you cannot find the essential feeling of belonging with your parents, you will naturally seek a sense of "home" in other ways, for example, using what psychologists call transitional objects. Transitional objects are objects, such as a stuffed animal or a blankie, used to ease feelings of anxiety and aloneness, which you experienced as a result of your emotionally abusive parents. These objects could become your mental representation of real parents who would have provided you with a sense of security and comfort. For example, the dearest relationships I had as a child were the ones I shared with my stuffed animals. I imagined they loved, comforted, and protected me in the multitude of ways my parents did not. I parented them the way I desired to be parented, and they parented me back. I was their favorite person. They kept me safe and cared about my feelings. They were my best friends, my tribe. I spent a tremendous amount of time alone in my room thriving in my pretend world. I loved it there. My sweet fantasy world was much kinder than the world that existed right outside of my bedroom door.

The movie *Annie* and the *Little House on the Prairie* book series also served as pivotal transitional objects for several years of my childhood. I watched *Annie* every chance I could and had two of the songs on the record on repeat, because they sung validation into my painful places. The song "Tomorrow" gave me hope in life and in myself, and the song "It's the Hard-Knock Life" felt true to what I was living each day. Although I wasn't an orphan, I lived with the heart of one. Annie had the life I dreamed of. She was a strong girl who knew who she was. She had a strength, fearlessness, and independence that I did not, but so desperately wanted. What we shared was the same yearning: parents who loved us. When Annie was chosen for adoption, I fantasized that one day a compassionate adult would recognize my suffering. I wanted someone to take me out of the hell I was living in and give me the love, time, attention, nurturing, support, guidance, and emotional safety I needed, just like what happened to Annie. I would freeze with fear in the movie when Annie was crawling up the railroad tracks fighting for her freedom with her predators chasing her. Punjab saves Annie by helicopter at the very last moment before she would have met the psychological death of losing her freedom and life story to her predators. My fantasies and transitional objects were much better parents to me than my actual parents. Like Annie's predators, my parents abused their power over me.

> **Moment of truth:** If you find that you isolate yourself from others when under stress, this is a sign that you had to solve your problems alone when you were a child.

Devastating Lifelong Impacts of Emotional Debt (Abuse)

With severely character disordered parents, you sensed their lack of attachment early in your childhood. However, you lacked the psychological insight to process why your parents are the way they are. When your parents are self-centered and uncaring, your memory of them will look something like this: No matter what you did, good or bad, you were either overlooked or harshly criticized. Each moment of being overlooked or criticized chipped away at your sense of self-worth and contributed to potentially lifelong impacts such as the following.

Depression

Growing up in complete dysfunction leaves you feeling deeply sad. I would cry for hours as a child but only do so when I was alone. It was crystal clear that my emotions unnerved my parents. Falling into this type of depression terrified me. To this day, I can say I have experienced depths of sadness I was unaware human beings were capable of feeling. The kind of sadness I experienced was far more advanced than my ability to manage it. I feared once it started, it would not stop. It devoured me for many, many years. I knew I was not okay, and I also knew I was alone. I am sure many of you can relate.

Anxiety

When you are not emotionally supported as a child by your parents, you are left without an advocate, lobbyist, and supporter. Without this, you have no model for how to stand in support of yourself, rendering you defenseless in navigating the world at large. You also have the anxiety of being given the responsibility to be, when not knowing how to be, your parents' advocate, lobbyist, and supporter. That responsibility comes with the anxiety of not doing any of those things well enough to make them happy.

Apathy

When you have been raised to be believe you are not a meaningful and important part of this world, you lose any organic feelings of excitement for life, causing you to question, "What's the point?"

Failure to Thrive

Many survivors struggled in school and with friends. How could you be expected to thrive without the security of loving parents? When that essential piece is missing, navigating normal relationships, responsibilities, daily tasks, and stressors is nearly impossible.

Hyperactivity

One root cause of attention deficit/hyperactivity disorder (ADHD) is thought to be complex post-traumatic stress disorder (C-PTSD). C-PTSD, which I detailed in my book *Adult Survivors of Toxic Family Members* (Campbell 2022), is associated with inattentiveness, hyperactivity, and impulsivity (Walker 2013). I had all of these as child. I almost failed three different grades, not because I wasn't smart, but because I was misunderstood and emotionally unstable. What was labeled as "ADHD," for me, felt more like intense feelings of nervousness combined with fear. This combination of emotions created a feeling of electricity that coursed through my body. This electricity made it impossible to focus. I learned to hate myself for not having the control to make it stop. School is where my "ADHD" was the most obvious to others. However, I didn't need to go to school to learn the subjects being taught to supposedly help me with life. I, and many of you, wanted school to give me the skills to survive the life I went home to. Sadly, schools don't teach these.

Aggression

Feelings of rage and aggression are the natural response to emotional abuse. Many of you likely started showing anger and despondency in the middle-school years. Honestly, all most of you wanted was to be heard. The more your feelings were dismissed, the louder, more frustrated, and angrier you naturally became. Instead of validating your grievances, your parents pushed you off as a "bratty teenager." I have heard many people describe feelings of aggression to such a degree that they daydreamed about destroying their parents. Yet, under that aggression was unimaginable hurt and the desire to be treated with basic human consideration.

Avoidance of Emotional Closeness

When your parents showed a lack of interest in you, close family and friends tended to follow along, viewing you as "troubled." The desire for emotional closeness under these coercive conditions placed you at too great a risk for replicating the excruciating rejection you lived through each day in your home. Avoiding closeness became the safer, albeit lonelier, alternative.

Increased Likelihood of an Eating Disorder

Eating disorders most often start in adolescence but can manifest at any point in life. Most eating disorders, at their core, are used to establish a feeling of agency over one's worth and daily existence.

Emotional Loneliness

A parent's most significant job is to fill your love tank, teaching you how to love yourself when they are not in your presence. When your childhood is filled with being incessantly yelled at, told what to do, neglected, and emotionally picked apart, you do not develop skills to self-soothe. Instead, you learn to self-abuse.

Healing the Wounds of Emotional Debt

Here are some ways to heal the wounds of emotional debt.

Clarify Your Feelings for Yourself

When you find yourself as an adult creating a slideshow to explain reality to your parents, this impulse to overexplain comes from fear. Overexplaining is a form of pleading for love. To disrupt this pattern, get clear on how you feel for yourself. Don't judge your emotions—just allow yourself to feel what you feel.

Express Your Feelings Rather Than Keeping Them In

Developing healthy relationships requires the risk of expressing yourself. You need to experience the ways in which other people respond to how you feel and what you need, so you can make wise choices in the company you choose to keep.

Soothe Yourself

If you grew up emotionally abused, you likely never learned to self-soothe. When I was a new mom, I learned that babies are best soothed through their five senses. This is a great place to start when learning to soothe yourself as an adult. Here are some examples.

Touch   You can access healing touch from the people you love, pets, or comfort objects like a weighted blanket or a soft afghan.

Taste   A cup of warm herbal tea can help you relax.

Smell   Aromatherapy with the use of bath salts, essential oils, body sprays, or even aromatic teas can decrease feelings of fear and stress.

Sight   Getting outside and seeing nature promotes a more spiritual view of life and is soothing to the soul. Looking at art or photos or watching your favorite movies can give your mind and heart a break from being in survival mode.

Sound   Music is therapy for many of us. Some people enjoy podcasts, while others choose sound-blocking earphones or white noise to create a space of peace and quiet.

Self-Soothing Can Help You Heal

Self-soothing is a beautifully engaging practice to invest in over the course of healing your life. As you heal, it becomes clear that emotional abuse and manipulation lurked in the corners of every aspect of your parents' parenting. Self-soothing allows you to put that stress down for the time you are engaging in these practices. Be gentle with yourself as we continue to unpack the game of twisted, forced love you were raised in.

Moment of truth: Toxic parents believe it is their right to force you to love them.

CHAPTER 3

Love Cannot Be Forced

Survivors of parental emotional abuse experience the saying "Love thy father and thy mother" to be one of the most pervasive and destructive in our culture. Children are not here to be supportive emotional outlets used to feed their parents' egos or to build their parents' self-worth or good image. How is it that the responsibility of parents' behaviors or reputations is placed on a child, when a child loving their parents should come a distant second to the parents' love and genuine concern for their child? Character disordered parents assume their children come included with a natural supply of automatic love and devotion to them. This automatic love from a child to a parent is what makes them good parents? This makes no sense.

> **Moment of truth:** As a child, you are born dependent on your parents, but your potential to feel love for them must be earned.

Authentic Love Versus Forced "Love"

Authentic love doesn't present as anything other than love itself. Genuine love is experienced as an unrestricted deep feeling of affection for a person, place, or thing you enjoy. Forced love has nothing to do with love or any of its natural expressions of happiness, enjoyment, safety, or freedom, but rather masquerades as manipulation, gaslighting, emotional blackmail, financial abuse, forced compliance, guilting, and shaming. If your parents must force, blackmail, demand, punish, fear, shame, or guilt you into loving them, whatever you feel for your parents simply will not be love.

Manipulative Tactics Utilized to Force "Love"

Because emotionally abusive parents view you from a space of ownership, they view it as their right to force you to feel, do, and be as they please. This warped mindset disempowers you and feels nothing like love. This type of parenting weakens your ability to move away from the tight hold of your parents as you mature and naturally desire increased independence. This type of parenting is soul crushing to children.

Following are some of the manipulative tactics parents use to secure the ultimate power over you, to force "love."

"Because I Am Your Parent"

The statement "because I am your parent" is used as a calculating lie by emotionally abusive and manipulative parents that has deep consequential ramifications not only on you as their child, but also on society. Nearly every brutality present in cultures worldwide has, in no small part, been enabled by a totalitarian mentality of obligations toward authority—in this case, what authoritarian parents call "love." Many of our cultural norms are based on obligations toward authority. This stems from the same mindset of manipulating people into a role of servitude based on a morally false, imposed obligation. This can be seen in the case of Britney Spears under the despotic hand of her father's imprisoning conservatorship, where he not only had control over her finances and estate but also her person. He, for his own distorted reasons, placed his daughter into emotional, physical, financial, psychological, and spiritual slavery "because he was her parent."

When your parents lack compassion, they cannot teach you the virtue of love. "Love" from their perception looks like service (servant) or good behavior (obedience). The demand behind the statement "because I am your parent" is strong-armed and lacks common sense. Its only basis is the position of your parents' relative authority over you.

Health Problems

Toxic parents are Machiavellian when it comes to manipulation as they joyously manufacture their afflictions by largely exaggerating minor illnesses or injuries to control you. They engage in these histrionics to avoid responsibility, block your ability to separate from them, and provoke the fear of "death abandonment" in you. These parents constantly talk openly about their illnesses and visit various medical professionals. Some will go as far to start GoFundMe accounts for themselves. They crave the worried concern in the eyes of their children and others, wrongly perceiving this as love.

Another way to use illness to force your "love" is when your manipulative parents overly focus on the state of your health, overexaggerating your symptoms. To keep you clinging to them for security and safety, they induce fear in you that your life and health are veering into dangerous territory. Your parents crave your desperation and are vain enough to view your fearful clutching to them as an expression of your love. This is emotional abuse.

Silent Treatment

The silent treatment is a tyrannical form of torment dysfunctional parents use to make you feel that your existence is meaningless. The coldness of their silence is powerful enough to produce emotional pain far more excruciating than a physical wound. To be sadistically silenced by your source of security is nothing short of traumatic, which is exactly why your parents use this method. They started the silent treatment in your early childhood and maintained this as a normal part of their repertoire of ways to manipulate you. As you reached your teenage years and developed a stronger mind of your own, the silent treatment intensified, with some of you having been completely ignored for days or weeks on end.

To disrupt the silent treatment, you may have tried bridging the gap by doing extra on top of what you normally did to gain approval. Children come to erroneously believe that if they could have been better children, they would have had better parents. It makes no sense that parents put the burden of change onto their children.

> **Moment of truth:** It seems odd that as a culture we hold children to a higher standard of maturity than the parents who are raising them.

Being silenced left many of you to spend an extraordinary amount of time alone as you waited for the silent but deadly hate-storm to pass. However, being alone and trying to handle a rejection that you could not understand was not a safe option either. In the aloneness and intensity of what felt like a pure hatred and disgust toward you, without any refuting guidance, you likely started developing the erroneous belief that your parents' hatred of you was justified. Those periods of enduring their silence were the seeds of the development of an ingrained belief that you are a worthless person. Whatever strategy you used to bridge the gap of silence, your parents interpreted your submission to their will as love.

Financial Security

Money, an abusive and manipulative parent's greatest love, gave them too much power over an already dependent person.

Here are some examples of parental financial abuse and negative ways financial abuse can affect you.

Examples of Financial Abuse

Examples of parental financial abuse include:

- threatening to cut you off when you hold a different opinion from theirs

- giving gifts as a license to control your behavior and decisions

- tracking every penny spent on you and using those costs to blackmail you

- requiring you to ask permission or to justify your own personal spending, even when it's your own money

- opening your bank statements and bills without your permission

- sabotaging your ability to educate yourself about finances or seek meaningful employment

- expecting you to use their credit card and bank account rather than getting your own

- paying bills for you, then guilting you afterward

- pressuring you to remain living with them

- criticizing or minimizing your choice of work

- pressuring you to quit your job

Negative Effects of Financial Abuse

Negative effects of financial abuse can include:

- feeling you do not deserve support

- having no concept of how to receive without feeling guilty, embarrassed, or ashamed

- becoming hyperindependent, refusing to accept help from anyone

- developing a fear of money

- seeing yourself as helpless and clueless about how to become more financially independent

Moment of truth: You want to believe your parents will follow through on their word because you mean something to them, not as a way to keep you indebted to them.

Hypocrisy

Emotionally abusive parents mold their life around a set of contradictions that place you in no-win situations. Those no-win situations force your dependency ("love") by keeping you too off-balance to reason through the emotional circus they create. When you were a child, hypocrisy made you crave a love and stability you would never receive. Following are some of the contradictions manipulative parents use to frustrate and weaken your resiliency.

Appear Exceedingly Self-Confident but Are Deeply Unstable

Your parents' denial of their own insecurity was responsible for the advanced melodramas they used to feign confidence whenever needed. They were performers, not genuine people. They overcompensated by wearing a fake personality of contrived kindness, hoping their charm would camouflage their cruelty. Their theatrics may have fooled others, but over time they stopped fooling you.

Remedy: Trust the truth of your own experience and live your life from that truth, even if it's just quietly within your own heart. Others will eventually catch on to the fake personas of your emotionally abusive and manipulative parents.

Expect Special Treatment but Resent Having to Give Back

Self-absorbed parents believe life and people, especially their children, require far too much from them. For them, giving is not about love or generosity. Giving has one sole purpose for them: scorekeeping.

Remedy: One of the greatest gifts you can give yourself is dropping all expectations for your selfish parents to be genuinely loving or generous toward you. When you surrender to this, you have more power to manage your reactions to things being given and then intentionally withheld for coercion.

Seek Out Targets

Emotionally abusive parents cannot function without a target to pester. For example, they may pursue legal actions, revenge, or no-win disputes for years. Should you question them, they will double down on control and turn a simple question into a war that you will lose.

Remedy: If you have no choice but to be under the care of your parents, it is best not to challenge them. Learning to be silent about what you know is correct will prove to be a superpower when dealing with your parents. This is because they do not care what you know. It will not matter to them how correct you may be or what refuting evidence you possess to prove your point. I am not encouraging you to lose your voice. I am encouraging you not to waste it.

Are Desperate for Attention

Your parents' gluttonous need for attention makes them extremely impatient when listening to or empathizing with you. Their motto is: "Enough about me, what do you think about me?" They thrive in the victim role and expect you to bend over backward to make sure their emotions and needs are the center of your attention.

Remedy: Avoid conversation as much as possible and cut conversations short when they occur. The less access your parents have to your emotions, the more peace you will have.

Are Quick to Blame yet Refuse to Own Their Own Part

Manipulative parents pass blame onto their children with lightning-fast reflexes. They assert that it was you who caused them to be a bad parent. They will not take accountability or show remorse for their actions.

Remedy: No matter what blame your parents cast your way, it does not mean you have to absorb that blame as valid. Come to trust that you know when you're being unfairly targeted.

Demand Loyalty but Don't Reciprocate

Toxic parents consistently test your loyalty to them yet have no issue exposing or humiliating you when it suits them.

Remedy: Don't expect your parents to reciprocate any loyalty. Instead, learn to be loyal to yourself.

Mock You but Don't Own It

Toxic parents use incessant sarcasm, taunting, and mocking to make you feel insecure. When confronted about their cruelty, they will not admit to their savage vindictiveness. Instead, you will be met with rage at your audacity to question their intentions.

Remedy: Keep the important things about your life private to protect your peace and avoid their mocking criticisms.

Use Hypocritical Parenting to Weaken Your Spirit

The goal of hypocritical parenting is to weaken your spirit. The weaker you are, the less confidence you have to pursue a separate life of your own. Emotionally abusive parents view your dependence on them as devotion, which allows them to continue living out their authority and control in your life. The audience of your life will have no idea of the manipulative atrocities happening behind closed doors. Outsiders dangerously assume, without proof, that things in your home are perfect because as a culture we have collectively bought into the canned image of exceptional parents. Most cannot fathom how painful it is to be trapped in what feels like an emotional prison. Selfish parents do not want you to become your own person, making them someone whom you can live without.

Trying to Force Your "Love"

Highly dysfunctional parents view love more as an object than a feeling. When love is perceived as an object, it is mistreated and mismanaged. What these parents fail to recognize is that love in its purest expression cannot be bought, forced, manipulated, or taken away. Egocentric parents try to demand and force "love" from you not because it is an emotion they feel, but because it's one they feel entitled to have. They like the way love looks from the outside as an image, but do not consider what it takes to earn, create, or sustain love. It is impossible to fill your loveless parent up with an emotion that holds no value to them. Yet, when nothing you do provides them the image of the love they seek, they lash out with disappointment that you have let them down and demand you continue searching for new ways to make them appear loved by you. You are to show the world how much you love them, so they can masquerade as good parents with a happy home and perfect children.

A young girl shared that she had put heart emojis next to her mom's name in her cell phone but did not have heart emojis next to her dad's name. Her dad, who was incredibly invasive of her privacy, would periodically go through her phone to see what went on between her and her mom. When he noticed the difference in emojis, he took it upon himself to add heart emojis next to his name. He told this young girl he did this because it looked like she loved her mom more than she loved him. Clearly, toxic parents are empty of all the things you need to sustain feeling alive, worthy, and happy. Your inability to fill your parents' emptiness becomes your emptiness.

Moment of truth: Your parents' job is not to force or control your emotions. It is their job to effectively manage their own.

Parental Empty-Cup Syndrome

Highly dysfunctional parents have what I call *parental empty-cup syndrome*. This is not a clinical term, but rather a term I created for the visual and psychological benefit of understanding who and what you are dealing with in your parents. Here are how the rules flow: Your parents are free to criticize, voice their opinions, ask anything of you no matter how invasive or inappropriate, and be rude, cruel, moody, unpredictable, and insensitive.

You are to follow through with no questions asked. The rules also dictate that you are not allowed to point out their bad behaviors, disagree, stand up for yourself, or say no to their demands. If you confront them on their contradictions, their bad behaviors suddenly become your fault. They retaliate by calling you crazy, difficult, selfish, dishonest, abusive, ungrateful, and mentally unstable.

Selfish and controlling parents refuse to give their children options around personal choice. Instead, they have an inflexible definition of family and what a good child should be. This lack of elasticity drives the dysfunction. For you to be loved, they see it as your responsibility to live up to their perfect image of you. These types of parents are not nurturing, attuned role models. They expect you simply to "be good" on your own. Yet, logic would tell you that in order to learn how to behave, children need their parents to be healthy role models. This can't happen when your parents are severely personality disordered. When the only position you are allotted in the relationship is that of the silent partner, it will drive you to deeply dislike your parents. Emotionally abusive parents are vengeful at their core. They seduce you into nonproductive, punitive conflicts to feed off your reactions to fill their emptiness. Following are some examples of how toxic parents retaliate to feast off your reactions.

Engage in Personal Attacks

Emotionally abusive parents establish dominance through the diminishment of your self-esteem. One way they do this is through personal attacks. For example, they blame you for other family members' problems, ridicule you over past mistakes, accuse you of not being a good child or family member, and consistently remind you of what they have sacrificed for you—thereby placing blame for their own feelings of unhappiness onto you. These types of parents say things like "How could you do this to me after all I've done for you?" The problem here isn't that your parents are or aren't fabricating what they feel. It is that your parents are using their feelings to assert dominance over you. This type of manipulation communicates that your emotions are fair game for personal attacks. Therefore, you would assume your parents should not be surprised when you respond to their attacks with unhappiness or anger.

A woman confronted her mother on her childhood abuse, and her mother retorted, "Well, I didn't know children had real feelings. How was I supposed to know that?" This mother absolutely knew her children had feelings because she saw the pain she caused in them. The pain she inflicted on her children replaced her feelings of emptiness with feelings of power.

Invalidate Your Feelings and Needs

When your parents aren't getting their way, they will attempt to invalidate your feelings and needs. For example, they may prevent you from talking, finish your sentences, change the subject when you're trying to express how you feel, push your needs off, intentionally cross your stated boundaries, act as if they know what you are thinking or feeling, minimize how you feel, and systematically work to change how you think and feel to line up with their ideals. This type of emotional cruelty is deadly on two fronts: First, it destroys the parent-child relationship by establishing an emotional hierarchy where your parents' feelings and needs are more important than yours. Second, it destroys your sense of importance—that sense that your feelings and needs are valid, individual, and important.

Withdraw Positive Interactions

The greatest weapon emotionally abusive and manipulative parents leverage is your desire for their love. Parental love is the most painful thing for any child to fear losing, which is why this is their weapon of choice. At any sign of you veering from their image of perfection, you will swiftly lose their warmth, praise, connection, and acceptance. These things are replaced with contempt, disgust, threats of being cut off, accusations of betrayal, and threats of losing the respect and love of all your other family members, friends, and any other person who may cross your path.

Withdraw Support

When your parents feel they are losing control, they will withdraw emotional and financial support, for the sole purpose of creating feelings of instability in you. If your parents are so willing to irrationally abandon you, it creates a state of terror around your survival and sets you down a path to feeling deeply insecure. Under these conditions, compliance is your only choice, until you're independent enough to fend for yourself.

The rules that govern parental empty-cup syndrome also include the rule that your parents are not required to take personal accountability for their own horrific acts. Being raised like this may cause you to experience any of the following.

Try to Fix Everything

You have been conditioned to feel a sense of terror that if you don't fix or comply with the demands of your parents, then you are hurting and betraying them. You are expected to respond to your abuse with maturity and perfection, while also having to predict and assume what your parents need without clear direction.

Remedy: You were not put on this planet for the sole purpose of taking care of parents who do not take care of you. You have a whole other divine reason for being here. This faulty programming is hard to undo. However, whatever was learned can be unlearned. The more you stay ahead of your automatic impulse to fix everything by staying in your own lane, the better able you become at extinguishing it.

Overapologize

One of the only avenues to peace with your parents was to apologize for things you did not do, or rather for offenses your parents acted out on you. When you apologized to your parents, it filled their empty cup, but you were left feeling as if everything was your fault. This habit of over-apologizing can last long into adulthood.

Remedy: It can be harder to quell the overapologizing habit than you may think. Confusion is the reason. Under your crass parents, you were consistently accused of being wrong when you had done nothing wrong. Because of this, it became challenging to know when you were actually wrong. To settle this confusion and help reestablish a sense of emotional peace between yourself and them, you falsely assumed you must have been wrong. This was not healthy, because it did not help you create boundaries. To establish a healthier way of showing up in relationships, practice apologizing only when you believe you have done something wrong. For example, change saying "I'm sorry I can't make it tonight" to "Unfortunately, I can't make it tonight." These small actions will help eliminate the overapologizing habit. They will also help you develop the confidence to start saying things such as "When you did [blank], it made me feel [blank], and I don't like that feeling." This way, people are given the opportunity to learn and honor your limits.

Struggle to Set Boundaries

Asserting boundaries proves difficult when you were never given the freedom to set them. Being forbidden to express yourself caused you to lose yourself. Because your parents operated in such a caustic manner, it naturally ate away at your desire for freedom and destroyed your self-confidence. Your individuality disappeared by force. The message your toxic parents gave was: if you dared to go off and live your own life, that your doing so would destroy theirs.

Remedy: You were born to be individual and unique. If this was not the case, there would be no need for a human body to physically separate one human being from another. You are separate, and your individuality is your destiny. To heal, make a list of the things you have dreamed about in private that your parents never would have approved of. As an adult, embrace your personal right to start living this list.

Take on the Role of Parent

Emotionally abusive and manipulative parents rob you of your childhood by thrusting you into the parent role, making you the caretaker of their emotions and problems. For example, when my mother went through one of her divorces, I was asked to confront her husband, which I did. I was asked to accompany her to her appointments with her attorney, which I did. She placed me in a role of responsibility where I had to act as her mother, best friend, and therapist. I did all she asked because she was my mom and I loved her. She manipulated me to believe she desperately needed me.

She wanted me to make her then-husband feel bad for cheating on her. After confronting him in person, I was upset. I went home in tears and smashed a family photo on the ground, which broke the glass in the frame. I left it on his doorstep to show him the family he destroyed. I wanted him to see the hurt. I did this for my mother. My mother knew I had left the frame. She felt he deserved it until he called and told her that my doing this scared him. My mother swiftly turned on me, telling me I had "gone too far." I had just confronted this man by myself, as a young adult. For a little broken frame to be used to make me believe I was a sick and twisted person made my head spin. I was doing as she asked. I wanted to help my mother from my whole heart. However, she was simply using me to do her dirty work, so I would get blamed for punishing her husband, and she could remain the victim. It took me years to unpack and understand this horrible act of thrusting me into the role of being her parent that she placed upon me.

Remedy: Take the appropriate steps to stop parenting your parents. They are adults and should be taking care of themselves, including their own personal, relationship, and financial matters, and most importantly taking care to protect you from unnecessary emotional stress. State your limits by saying, "I will no longer be handling these types of problems for you." Expect a tantrum to follow. Ignore it and keep your boundary. This is exactly how healthy parents would handle the unnecessary complaining and demands from their children. The mindset to hold is that if your parents, or anyone for that matter, can reasonably do something on their own, you should let them.

Worry That People Are Mad at You

Having been raised by emotionally abusive parents, many of you will fear that anyone you love will suddenly find fault with you and become angry. From this fear, you may reflexively seek reassurance in your relationships far more than is necessary, making you seem insecure to those who couldn't possibly understand the basis of your fears. The idea that someone is mad at you can be enough to paralyze your ability to function.

Remedy: To decrease persistent worries, remind yourself that assumptions are made-up stories in your head based on fears, not facts. In the healthy world, everyone is innocent until proven guilty. So often, as a trauma survivor, you may imagine the worst-case scenario that someone is mad at you. As a result, you're likely to launch into hypothetical conversations in your head about why a person may be angry with you, envisioning yourself desperately trying to fix the mystery thing that you did. You fear that if you don't repair things, you will lose the relationship. When you fall down this rabbit hole, remind yourself never to assume.

The Natural Development of Internalized Resentment

The concept of "family" under highly dysfunctional parenting is the epitome of the word "cult" in culture—the family culture must stick together under one rule, no variance, or you face abuse, rejection, and abandonment. A human being can take only so much for so long before the accumulated abuses and manipulations start creating an intense feeling of resentment inside of you.

There is no way to survive under a conflict-saturated, conquer-and-divide parenting model other than through obedience, which leads to the building of accumulated resentments. You can feel only so much agitation and worry before it throws you into the depths of resentment for having to feel so much pain. Resentments can be expressed outwardly and inwardly. You can outwardly erupt at the parent who is stepping all over you, which leads to them shaming you. Or you can internalize your feelings and act your frustrations out on yourself through experiences such as cutting, eating disorders, road rage, substance abuse, or some other form of self-sabotage.

Most of you learned this one the hard way. After being provoked into one angry response after another, you got labeled "out of control" and told you need to "get it together." You "got it together" by having to stuff your anger deep inside to appear good on the outside, which was all your parents cared about. They did not care about you. They cared about appearances. It is easy to become resentful when you're persistently forced away from being yourself. When parents base their idea of love on expectations that you were born to fill their inner emptiness and uphold their image of family, they are consistently placing an empty cup in front of you and demanding that you fill it, even when it is not psychologically possible for you to do so.

It seems, as a society, we are far more concerned with the reputation and appearances of parents than we are with the protection of children. We turn a blind eye to the suffering of young children and adult children to avoid bringing shame upon the parents who abuse them. How does this make sense?

Your parents never should have given you the responsibility to know how to navigate their mood swings, tempers, and/or disorders. The emotional games egocentric parents play are used to incite guilt when you feel resentment toward them. Guilt is a silent but deadly emotional weapon. When you live in guilt, even the smallest things feel like huge issues, because those small things are layered on top of preexisting trauma. Wanting to be your own person and feeling resentful because you have never been allowed this is a healthy response to problematic parenting. Becoming your own person is not something you should have been made to feel guilty about. In the next chapter, we are going to unpack any feelings of guilt you were manipulated to carry in wanting to be your own, separate, and free person from your grossly immature parents.

> **Moment of truth:** Egocentric parents equate your desires for autonomy as antifamily.

CHAPTER 4

Transforming
Maladaptive Guilt

Guilt is an intense emotional reaction to a perceived failure to live up to your own or another's imposed standards. Unlike other emotions, such as mad, sad, glad, afraid, ashamed, or hurt, guilt must be learned. Healthy parents utilize guilt when necessary and appropriate to help you learn the critical importance of developing a healthy conscience. Emotionally abusive and manipulative parents use guilt as their primary form of parenting, causing the guilt they induce to transmute into the deeper and even more paralyzing feelings of shame and worthlessness to keep you disempowered and in need of their approval. For many of us, myself included, our parents used guilt as their go-to pattern of communication.

When Guilt Is a Weapon

Guilt, as it relates to fear, has long been a tool utilized by emotionally abusive parents. Guilt is profoundly effective because it spreads from person to person, like a virus. When one sibling sees another sibling being emotionally controlled or berated, they feel guilt and fear. When a child hears a parent speak terribly about other family members behind their back, they feel guilt and fear. When a child sees one parent attack another parent, they feel guilt and fear. When a child witnesses a parent having road rage or public rage, the child feels guilt and fear.

My father was a rage-alcoholic and not only was he violent with me as a child, but I also witnessed him lose his mind and physically harm others, for example, due to road rage or a neighbor dispute. I will never forget him punching a snowplow driver in the face because his blade hit a rock hidden by the snow, which made his snowplow swerve into the middle of the road. To avoid an accident, my father had to swerve, and our car went into a ditch. My father, enraged out of his mind, got out of the car and forced this terrified young man to push our car out of the ditch by himself while my father watched. The man was crying and apologizing. My father didn't care. He never did. Everything was always someone else's fault. He viewed his insane reactions to people as justified. Witnessing him abuse this man terrified me as I watched this man's tears and blood run down his face. I was so scared for my dad to get back in the car that I was visibly shaking from adrenaline. When he asked me why I was shaking, I felt guilty, so I lied and told him I was cold. I sat in silence as he drove me home rattling on and on about what an idiot that "Mexican man" he had just abused was. He had no remorse. I resented him for placing me in these dangerous and scary situations, then I felt guilty for feeling resentful. Scary, threatening, unpredictable, violent parents create intimidated children.

Threat-Based Parenting

Under abusive and manipulative parents, everything is a threat, and yet somehow you brought it on yourself. They systematically reduce you to be a person who only does as they are told. You are left not knowing how to make decisions without first checking in with your parents. Why? Because the fear they instilled in you interferes with your capacity to think rationally and independently. It has you living in a twisted state of moral perfectionism. When you suffer from moral perfectionism, you panic at the thought that maybe you have done something even remotely wrong, causing you to obsess over your perceived mistakes and flooding you with guilt and anxiety. This overpowering guilt and anxiety make you seek an unrealistically clean moral state of mind.

Moment of truth: Toxic parents groom you to feel so afraid of disappointing them that you learn to make decisions that go against what is in your best interest.

An example is a family where the father had complete control over both his children. He would show up at their athletic events and train them apart from their coach and team members. He had to be at the center of everything his children did and demanded they each consult him on every area of their life. To this day, as adults, they remain at his beck and call. This father keeps his children close because their mother died tragically when they were young, and the mother's family largely saw him as a contributing party in her death. To camouflage his role in their mother's illness and unhappiness, he became "super dad" to make up for his lack of being a decent and kind husband. He used his "devoted father" image to assuage his guilt and any culpability he held around their mother's passing. He has made his children totally dependent upon his approval and holds a godlike status in their mind. He has interfered in their romantic relationships, with the raising of their children, and in their overall development as adults. Both believe they must check in with him for his "daily wisdom and guidance," or they fear disappointing him.

Far too many parents justify and excuse the fear and guilt they intentionally inflict on their children under the guise of "I do this because I love you." You abuse me because you love me? That makes no sense. When you are told that your parents' love for you was the cause for them abusing you, it sets the stage for a lifetime of confusion around what love is. Understandably, it can prove difficult to locate love, recognize it, embrace it, accept it, understand it, feel comfortable in it, or trust it as an adult. That is what happens when you learn to equate love with pain.

Healthy Versus Toxic Guilt

One of my favorite sayings is "Not all guilt is created equal." As mentioned above, a certain amount of guilt is necessary for the development of a healthy conscience. The type of healthy guilt that helps you develop a healthy conscience is called *adaptive guilt*. With adaptive guilt, you learn through your own experience. When you do something wrong, your adaptive guilt alerts you to where you erred, opening an opportunity for you to understand what you may need to change to avoid repeating the experience that made you feel badly. An example of adaptive guilt would be unintentionally taking your bad mood out on someone you love. Once you see the hurtful ramifications of your actions, your feelings of guilt motivate you to take ownership of your misdirected mood onto the person you hurt and rectify your behavior, so that your relationship isn't permanently damaged. Adaptive guilt teaches you to think for yourself and to consider the feelings of others.

Maladaptive guilt is far different. It is toxic guilt. Maladaptive guilt develops when your parents emotionally intimidate you with no concern for how they may be destroying your self-worth and/or their relationship with you. For example, your mother wants you to talk to her on the phone at least three times per week. When this is too much for you to accommodate, she berates you for being a bad child, calling you a selfish person who doesn't care about family. In this example, you are left feeling guilty for no valid reason, causing you to make unhealthy changes to your own lifestyle to fulfill her needs and avoid her berating abuse. You have been conditioned to become overwhelmed with feelings of guilt any time you stand up for yourself instead of giving in to the impractical demands of your parents. You are essentially feeling guilty when you have not done something wrong. This is maladaptive guilt.

Development of a Savage Inner Critic

Maladaptive guilt is powerful enough to develop the voice of a savage inner critic. Your parents' critical, angry, snide, punitive, dismissive voice of complete disgust gets internalized as your inner critic. Your inner critic manifests through a running internal dialogue, giving you a daily, minute-by-minute narrative on everything you're doing wrong and all the ways in which you need to do better. Living in maladaptive guilt teaches you to sacrifice independent thought and believe that the happiness of your parents (or others) is predicated on your every move. Following are some effective ways to evict your parents from continuing to live on as your inner voice.

Speak a Language of Love to Yourself

Speak to yourself with compassion. Speak to yourself as you had always wanted your parents to speak to you.

Speak Bravery, Kindness, and Hope to Yourself

Tell yourself that you have what it takes to be, do, and achieve anything you set your mind to. Be your own advocate.

Speak Wisdom and Truth to Yourself

Listen to your gut instincts and learn to trust them. Always tell your truth. Live honestly, quietly, directly, and responsibly.

Become Your Own Safety Net

You may not realize it, but you know how to take care of yourself, or you would not have made it this far. Make sure you have a place to call home, food in the fridge, a journal to write in, and people to talk to.

Listen to Yourself

You know yourself better than anyone else. Give yourself some credit and take the advice you would give to others in similar situations.

Become Your Own Emotional Home

Create a healing space in your environment. For example, I have turned my home office into a healing room. I found an artist whose paintings reflect my life story. I hung the artwork that depicts my pain on the back wall, to remind me that my pain is always behind me. In the middle of the room, I placed a giant love sac that resembles a womb to cuddle up in. This love sac is a place for me to feel safe, held, comfortable, and warm. To the side of my love sac is artwork that reflects my healing process today. There are two pieces, one depicting personal empowerment and the other empathy. On the wall in front of me is a painting of a woman with wild red hair holding the earth suspended above her hand. She represents the woman I am obsessed with becoming. When I need the feeling of parents, security, or home, I come to my healing room. In this room, I do not feel emotionally homeless.

> **Moment of truth:** When guilt is the overpowering relational tool used by your parents, it makes it nearly impossible to see yourself as good.

Working Through Maladaptive Guilt

To work through maladaptive guilt, you must identify the type of guilt you are feeling. Is the guilt you are feeling healthy and coming from your own insight and awareness? Or is the guilt being forced upon you by no fault of your own by someone outside of you? When you recognize feelings of maladaptive guilt, understand that what you are feeling isn't healthy. You can work to reject induced guilt by reminding yourself of the following.

- You do not need to take responsibility for feelings that are not yours to feel or actions that you did not take.

- You are not responsible for the problems or the unhappiness of parents who refuse to meet their own needs or take responsibility for their own feelings.

- It is your parents' choice to feel mad, angry, upset, or disappointed when they don't get their way.

- You do not need to feel guilty for things that never should have been your responsibility in the first place.

Maladaptive guilt is potent enough to burrow so deeply into your psyche that it shuts you off from joy. Some of you have been raised in such profound levels of maladaptive guilt that when someone gives you a genuine compliment, the first thing you wonder is what they want from you. To feel guilty when receiving a compliment, because you are programmed to question what you will owe that person for being kind or generous to you, is a horrible way to live. You deserve so much better.

Healing Exercise for Maladaptive Guilt

Remember that what you think determines how you feel, and how you feel determines your lived experience. Take a minute to check yourself when consumed with maladaptive guilt. To unpack this, try the following.

List the Things You Feel Guilty About

Write a list of the things that you feel maladaptive guilt about. Next, create a second list that counters every guilty thought written down on the first list. This type of exercise helps you recognize that there are alternative and healthier ways to look at things. Making lists assists you in untangling the dysfunctional thoughts that tether you to your trauma. Each time you feel guilty, you can revisit the new list that counters the maladaptive guilt list you learned to punish yourself with. The more you reinforce your new beliefs, the more your heart and head align with them, and the freer you allow yourself to feel. For example, when someone gives you a compliment, instead of thinking, *What do they want or expect from me?* you could say to yourself, *This person genuinely cares about me and doesn't need me to repay them for a compliment. I deserve the compliments I receive.*

Visualize Releasing Feelings of Maladaptive Guilt

Visualization is a powerful tool. I encourage you to take in a slow deep breath and close your eyes. Now, say out loud, "I release my parents and their toxic guilt from me physically, emotionally, mentally, spiritually, relationally, and financially." Then hold all that toxic guilt, as if it were cupped in your hand, and with a tossing motion envision letting it go into the Universe to be transformed and released from your spirit. Now, say out loud, "I release my parents from me to their highest good, whatever that may be."

Here are some helpful reminders to soothe your soul.

- Just because your parents say you are wrong does not mean they are right.

- Just because you're the child doesn't mean it's your job to be the family fixer.

- Just because your parents raised you doesn't mean your parents own you.

- You owe it to yourself and to those who love you to create distance from parents who abuse and manipulate you, and to do this guilt-free.

- You're doing the best you can with the circumstances you've been given, and you're doing a great job.

Children Do Not Owe Their Parents

It is a difficult and heartbreaking truth to acknowledge that not all parents are good parents. However, children do not choose their parents or the ways their parents treat them. Because having a child is a parent's choice, it would make sense that the more responsible, skilled, and mature parent would see themselves as owing it to their less skilled, more vulnerable child to be purposeful in treating their child with the upmost love, concern, and respect. In this healthy narrative, children have rights, and parents have obligations, rather than the opposite.

When you are a child raised in the opposite narrative, as many of you and I have been, the last thing you likely considered when grappling to understand your less-than-perfect behavior was to look at the trauma—how your parents treated you—that was causing it. Instead, the propagated myth assumes that all parents are good and that your bad behavior must be due to some type of flaw in you, such as mental illness, chemical imbalance, or other neurological problem. They may point to nutritional deficiencies or assume you are being negatively influenced by your peers. Toxic parents are not below making claims that you are like your "other parent." Many of you were told you were just like your father when your mother was unhappy with you—and told by your father that you were just like your mother when he wasn't happy with you. This is all guilt-driven thinking.

> **Moment of truth:** Children do not owe their parents their life simply because their parents gave life to them or chose to adopt them.

When none of these assertions adequately explains your behavior, parents move to blaming other factors, such as TV, music, the internet, and video games. Of course, the current sociopolitical factors will be added to the equation with your parents blaming your generation's politics for your behavior. It is not that these varying areas of influence combined bear no impact on behavior, but I find it interesting that at the very bottom of that list is to hold the parents' attitudes and behaviors toward their children as the most significant contributing factor. Why? Because parents being bad parents is not what our larger culture is willing to examine. Instead, there is a strong resistance to question the validity of such an assertion. The larger culture protects parents under the false belief that all is well in the Universe as long as parents aren't left having to take the proper accountability for their abusive parenting.

When parents use an abuse of power to govern their parenting practices, this is the epitome of corruption. Society needs to stop forcing children to feel obligated to maintain relationships with their emotionally abusive parents. This is not teaching children anything life-sustaining or healthy. It is not teaching children that family comes first. It is teaching children that regardless of how horrifically someone treats them, they are still to love those people unconditionally. For this reason and many more, society needs to stop forcing children to have relationships with emotionally abusive parents and to stop shaming them when they make the healthy choice to step away.

In our culture, it is fair game for parents to recruit their children to manage their emotions for them. Children take on this burden instinctively to protect their connection with their parents, but it's an awfully heavy and unfair burden for a child to carry. In refusing to see emotionally abusive parenting for what it is, we are forcing children to deal all alone with the traumatic effects that their disturbed parents have on them. We leave children unsupported, while we enable and protect parents because it is uncomfortable to tell parents they need to do better. This is inexcusable. Anyone who is complicit in a child's abuse is also contributing to it. Children need to be supported for setting the appropriate boundaries with parents, even when that means no contact.

Moment of truth: Not one child in this Universe should be made to feel they were asking for too much when they asked their parents for unconditional love, genuine acceptance, and meaningful accountability.

CHAPTER 5

Untwisting Their Demands for Respect

Children are taught from the youngest of ages to respect and honor their parents. This belief is included in the Ten Commandments and in some form in all religions. In healthy family systems, respect can be a wonderful concept to uphold. However, what happens to the child who is not respected or honored by their parents? Again, it begs the question, how does it make sense for parents to hold a child, who is far less skilled and mature, responsible for their problems rather than themselves? Yet, toxic parents get away with holding children accountable for their own problems all the time. As discussed earlier, this may safeguard society's need to protect parents, but it fails to address the real problem: bad parents. It seems strange and wrong to give abusive parents a public free pass, allowing them to hide in plain sight. Perhaps it's simply too painful to admit that abuse happens in our closest quarters and to the most innocent members of our human family: our children.

Respect as an Expression of Love

Self-aware parents desire to give their children a good experience of them as parents, including the ways in which they discipline. Conscious parents turn discipline into teachable moments. Healthy parents rarely, if ever, lose control when they are mad. Instead, they become serious and patient, quiet their voice, and communicate person-to-person in a safe setting.

They approach conflict with the desire for an explanation, rather than approaching it from an accusation. They see no value in yelling or hitting their children. They choose curiosity over chastisement, and progress over pride. They are interested to discover at what level their children have the capacity to think about their own thinking and behavior in any given situation, and the subsequent consequences of those things. They don't seek to control their children. They seek to guide them. Healthy parents are mindful that the stability of their children's personal and social development falls directly on how they treat them.

Healthy parents find little to no value in taking things away from their children as a method of punishment. They understand that children can learn to live without anything they take away, including removing the bedroom door from its hinges, confiscating a cell phone, or removing internet access. Children are resourceful and will find ways to get what they want as a means of asserting their own power in the relationship. In lieu of punishments and taking things away, self-aware parents hold open discussions, approaching their children with a "meeting of the minds." Healthy parents understand when two or more minds come together in connection that this creates a mastermind. Their goal is to establish mutual understanding to gain life lessons and create fair agreements. When it comes to discipline, healthy parents include their children in the deciding of consequences, allowing them the opportunity to become a master of their own mind. This type of mutual engagement between them helps children learn to think rationally and objectively about who they are and the results of their choices and actions. When children learn this, they reciprocate it.

Moment of truth: Parents who micromanage and criticize every detail of their child's life naturally place themselves on the receiving end of their child's resistance, bad attitude, dishonesty, and secrecy.

Respect as Obedience

Respect, taught as a concept of love, is not the version of respect severely character disordered parents show their children. Let's examine how manipulative parents misuse the concept of respect in their parenting.

"Respect" is the most weaponized word used by emotionally abusive and manipulative parents. They demand a type of respect that has nothing to do with respect at all. When children aren't "behaving," you will hear emotionally abusive parents lamenting about how "disrespectful their children are," how they "don't respect their rules," or that their children "have zero respect for adults." They use the concept of respect to establish "good guys" and "bad guys." Highly dysfunctional parents have the immature expectation that children respecting them is automatic, not a character trait that must be learned, modeled, nurtured, or earned. Yet, under the delusion that respect is inborn, there could be only perfect children. When this simplistic belief system of respect proves false, this is when emotionally abusive parents become dehumanizing toward their children. They apply rules to their children they do not live themselves, then demand to be respected. Consequently, it seems logical that these types of parents raise children who have little to no respect for them.

Abusive and manipulative parents do not view respect as emotional—something to be felt—but rather as behavioral—something to demand. They do not care if you *feel* good. They care that you *act* good. You may have outwardly obeyed your parents to placate them, but this response is about survival, not respect. Living in survival mode fills you with such intense feelings of inner turmoil that you naturally reach a limit where you cannot hold in your angry feelings anymore. That anger eventually gets directed at the source, who then chastises your reaction and swiftly accuses you of being the (disrespectful) problem. A major point of emotional abuse is to make the victim (child) think they are abusing the abuser (parent). Parents such as this are deeply offended by anyone who looks out for themselves or stands up for what they believe in. Yet, true to their duplicity, they do not want to look out for anyone other than themselves, and this includes their children. This type of parenting leaves children with little other choice than to start lying and hiding to protect themselves. Lying becomes a strategy for coping. Lying or withholding information gives children a taste of the personal freedom they crave without getting in trouble. However, if their secrets are caught by their parents, children are belittled, called liars, and have their most prized possessions taken away to punish them. At the same time, they are branded disrespectful. Children who are shown zero respect come to deeply despise their parents.

Ways Toxic Parents Disrespect Their Children

Here are some ways toxic parents can disrespect you.

Ask Too Many Questions

Being barraged with questions does the opposite of making you feel open to your parents when the questions themselves are accusatory. What you needed was a parent who had faith in you, to demonstrate respect for you in a way that would inspire you to be open with them.

Are Quick to Judge

When you did share something private, your parents may have responded with "I told you so" or "How could you be so stupid?" Or they attacked every detail of what you shared and immediately lost your trust because they made trusting them unsafe.

Invade Your Personal Space

Toxic parents do not grow with you as you are naturally maturing in your development. These types of parents still want to wipe your nose, pick you up and swing you around, or hug and kiss in ways that are not comfortable.

Talk over You

Egocentric parents speak *over, to, for,* or *at* you. They do not speak *with* you because they are uninterested in hearing you. This makes it difficult to work though the struggle of finding your own unique answers to life's questions. When parents suffocate you with a flood of words, you are robbed of experiencing your personal significance, which is essential to develop confidence.

Encroach on Your Independence

One goal of healthy parenting is to raise children who are not easily influenced to succumb to the pressures of others. When your parents show a belligerent lack of respect for your privacy or the decisions you want and need to make for yourself, by pressuring you to go against yourself to bend to their way, nothing good can come from that.

Emotionally abusive and manipulative parents fail to understand that children questioning rules and traditions they are expected to automatically adhere to is a sign of intelligence and a strong sense of individuality. Healthy parents do not view unquestioned obedience as a sign of "goodness." Healthy parents do not want to raise children who are incapable of thinking for themselves, making them easy for others to manipulate.

> **Moment of truth:** When your parents make you feel valued and capable, you are less likely to engage in power struggles.

When you are not given or shown respect from your parents, it has a deeply negative impact on your self-belief. Here are some truths.

- You deserved parents who honored your privacy.

- You did not deserve to be drilled with a billion questions.

- You deserved the space to learn on your own.

- You deserved to be heard, seen, and considered.

- It should have been your choice when, what, or whether you chose to share.

- You deserved parents who believed in your ability to problem-solve and succeed.

When these things were not present, any love you felt for your parents transmuted into feelings of repulsion and disgust. This also is not your fault. This is what your parents created. Parents who see their role as more superior to yours fail to think about how destructive they are and the intense feelings of dislike they cause you to feel toward them.

Here are some healthy mindsets to keep.

- You are not betraying your parents by acknowledging, speaking about, and trying to work through generational trauma. Rather, you are ensuring a new healthy legacy.

- You are worthy of much more than your parents made you feel. Sometimes it is necessary to show your worth through your absence.

- Sometimes when the people you love hurt you the most, it is better to stay quiet. If your love isn't enough, do you think your words will matter?

- When it comes to toxic parents, less is always more.

Just because parents have children doesn't put them at liberty to know everything about their children. This type of invasiveness demonstrates a blatant lack of respect for a child's individual rights. Every person, every human being, every child needs personal space to function optimally.

A Secret Garden of Privacy

Privacy is a critical element of respect. Every child deserves a secret garden. You deserved spaces in your life that were personal and private. With the advent of the internet, children today have a new arena where toxic parents can invade their privacy. Parents can require access to all passwords to social media and email accounts, spy on search histories, and claim to do all of this in the name of "protecting their kids." Emotionally abusive and manipulative parents take advantage of this kind of unlimited access to unabashedly control and gather information on their children for extortion. A lack of privacy kills love. It kills trust. It kills authenticity, and it kills honesty because when your parents overly control you, they kill your spirit. You start believing that your healthy curiosities and experimentations are despicable atrocities. You start questioning whether you are, in fact, an irreparable, vile human being.

For example, a teenage boy was becoming curious about girls. His abusive, invasive mother caught him looking up sexual topics on YouTube and flew into a rage about sex, how dirty it is, how disgusting he was to be thinking about it, and how dangerous it was to be looking it up online. She dramatically warned him he was on his way to becoming a sex addict. However, she was aware the appropriate parental controls were in place on his YouTube account and cell phone that would prevent him from seeing much of anything. After shaming her son, she cast her rage toward his father. This mother demanded the father "take care of it," threatening him not to have one of those "it's normal to look up sex, dude" conversations. Ironically, this mother was a woman who had been a model in her younger years, and nearly every photo taken of her modeling was overtly sexualized, including the clothes, the makeup, and the explicitly sexual expression on her face. How confusing is this?

Curiosity about sex is normal and natural for a teenager. The opportunity for a healthy conversation about sex, including the dangers and the joys, was completely missed. The shame and punishment this boy received was callous, deeply damaging, and uncalled for. There was not something wrong with this boy. There was something fundamentally wrong with the parenting. Being allowed a private life hidden from your own parents is healthy. Children need to have parts of their life that are no one else's business. Yet, toxic parents believe they have the right to control and manage every minute detail, often gaining access into what you hold private through spying or even baiting siblings or other relatives to expose and deceive you. When triangles are formed to invade your personal privacy, you feel even more violated, betrayed, and shamed knowing someone else you trusted needlessly ratted you out.

Healthy parents allow for privacy, viewing privacy as a beneficial and necessary personal right. There is no belief held that every detail of your life is their business. They keep lines of communication open. At the fore-front of a healthy parent's mind is: "If I were not my child's parent, would they respect me and choose to love me?" When a parent knows this answer would be yes, they can be confident they are doing a good enough job. Their child doesn't just love them; their child admires and respects them. For this type of connection to develop between child and parent, trust and emotional safety must be present. A common statement expressed by children raised by toxic parents is that if their parents weren't their parents, they would never choose to have them in their life. Most of us want people in our life who bring more peace than problems. Makes sense.

Children Need Peace to Thrive

Peace provides a feeling of inner harmony that is free from intrusion. Emotionally abusive parents do not provide peace. Raised under toxic parents, you don't feel peace. Instead, you feel the need to "keep the peace." Keeping the peace means staying out of your parents' way to avoid conflict. Sadly, in doing this, you are forced to sacrifice your truth and to stand in total betrayal of how you feel and what you know to be true for yourself, with no way to make any of what you feel real. Growing up like this, you know that something is horribly off. However, there is no avenue to make your experience tangible—something you can agree on, discuss openly, and find a solution for—when your parents won't listen to you because they are committed to discrediting you. In this system, the path to peace is to "keep the peace."

> **Moment of truth:** The most abusive parent in the family system is the least challenged or confronted.

Peace on the Outside

Keeping the peace has nothing to do with peace itself. Keeping the peace is motivated by worry. When there is no peace, navigating the relationship with your parents equates to constantly walking on eggshells, which is stressful. You are acutely aware that no matter what you do or don't do, there will be a cost. Therefore, before doing anything, you engage in the mental gymnastics of overassessing what it will cost you to do or say anything in support of yourself and weigh your options. With toxic parents, the only option for peace is to do what you need to do to avoid conflict with them. This is not having a childhood. This is being robbed of your childhood.

Defensive Hypervigilance Trauma

When you have been forced to keep the peace, you grow to be reflexively anxious from too many occasions of being unfairly blamed for wrongs you did not do. You are forced to confess to imagined or supposed misbehaviors that did not occur. Everything you do and don't do is used as blackmail to keep you under your parents' control. Peace is impossible when you live in a chronic state of self-protection. This type of chronic defensiveness is what I have coined *defensive hypervigilance trauma*. It is my belief that defensive hypervigilance trauma comes from the deep-seated fear of being consistently viewed as bad. Defensive hypervigilance trauma causes you to constantly live on alert, trying to predict potential dangers or threats, real or made-up. The loss of your voice forces you to keep the depths of the stress you feel buried inside, causing you to misread the environment outside your family, where you find yourself feeling defensive in situations where you are not being personally attacked.

This is what living in chaos does to damage the human spirit. When attempts to advocate or defend yourself have been systematically attacked as talking back, you are not being treated in an equitable manner. Psychologically abusive parents demand you "Don't. Talk. Back." Ironically, talking back would imply a two-person conversation. The only type of conversation a dysfunctional parent will have is a "their-way" conversation. In a their-way conversation, you are always wrong.

Ways to Heal from Defensive Hypervigilance Trauma

Here are ways to heal defensive hypervigilance trauma.

Know Your Triggers and Anticipate Them

Having an awareness of what your triggers are and when or with whom they are likely to pop up allows you to prepare better responses for when you're in a difficult situation. For example, if you know your parent will predictably rage a terrible mood on you, you can plan for this situation. You may decide in advance that you're going to use your feet to remove yourself from the situation when it happens, or that you're going to take a few deep breaths, shut your mouth, and do what your parent is demanding to protect yourself from further degradation.

Moment of truth: Sometimes the best way to protect yourself in the moment is to allow your parent to think they have won.

Name Your Feeling

When you feel a sudden increase in your blood pressure, or you find your anxiety is on a slow build, causing you to feel sweaty, sad, scared, and shaky, these physical responses can alert you to label what you are feeling. When you are aware of these physical changes and name what you're feeling (such as frustrated, irritated, sad, or angry), it orients you to your body and makes it easier to manage your emotions.

Use Explanation Rather Than Reverse Accusation

When you are being unfairly attacked by your parent, assume they do not have all the information they need and do what you can, if they allow you to speak, to fill them in. Use this tactic instead of getting defensive and pointing fingers back at them, which will only fuel the fire.

Know It's Not You

How your parent treats you says more about them and their own lack of self-control than it says anything real or valid about you. See them for who they are, know it won't change, and work to not engage in their dramatics.

Adopt a Growth Mindset

In whatever ways you can, grab the lessons from each painful experience. Each day, you can let your parents inspire you in a direction of who and how you never want to be.

Apply Self-Compassion

Show yourself the same kindness, care, and concern you crave from your parents. Self-compassion helps shift your focus from default survival-mode behaviors of defensiveness to a more open, receptive state, allowing you to better manage your more reactive tendencies.

Try Gray-Rocking

Gray-rocking is a technique where you become the most unresponsive and boring person in relationship with your parents to stay out of their line of fire. Examples of gray-rocking include avoiding eye contact, maintaining a flat tone of voice, staying a safe physical distance, keeping your answers to questions brief, and deflecting the conversation back to your parent.

Peace on the outside comes through utilizing these techniques to quell your defensiveness. As you master keeping the peace on the outside, you will develop the courage to start setting the necessary boundaries to begin establishing peace on the inside.

Peace on the Inside

Peace on the inside is a whole different kind of peace. Inner peace is natural, free, and aligned with the essence of the human spirit. It develops from voicing your feelings and setting necessary boundaries. When you have peace on the inside, you take care of your own emotions by communicating with the source of your pain about what you will and will not tolerate. Thereby, you value yourself, even when or if that means losing the relationship. In essence, when you set boundaries, your intention is to keep people in your life by letting them know where they have misstepped, so they can do better in the future. With peace also comes clarity, closure, joy, openness, vulnerability, healthy attachments, honesty, trust, tranquility, truth, and self-love. In healthy families, children are treated with the upmost admiration, and their lines of tolerance are honored and protected. Children who are encouraged to use and honor their voice nearly always want to maintain close emotional connections with their parents. They have been given inner peace.

If you genuinely want to honor thy mother and thy father, aren't you doing exactly this with your boundaries? Think about the personal choice each of us, including your parents, has to be ourselves. Consider writing about this in a journal. Your parents make a choice to be abusers because that is who they are and how they want to show up and treat you. If you don't like this and you beg them to change, you are not honoring their choice to be the toxic and manipulative parent they choose to be. If the highest form of love is acceptance, then your setting boundaries on your abusive parents allows them to go on without you and live their best life as the abusive person they desire and choose to be.

CHAPTER 6

Overcome Your Self-Neglect

Growing up abused and manipulated extinguishes your inner light. The bulb is inside of you, but it isn't lit. And it's no wonder. You have been taught to turn that light off whenever you have needs, wants, thoughts, or feelings about anything your parents do not align with. In the heathy world of parenting, the needs of the child always come first, because this is what makes the most sense. In the perverse world of emotionally abusive and manipulative parenting, the needs of the parents supersede the needs of the child, who has a naturally greater need base. Toxic parents place the workload of the relationship and the establishment of peace solely on the child. Sadly, children like you and me were raised to believe that love required us to give up our sense of *self*, including self-respect.

Toxic Emotional Set Points That Lead to Self-Neglect

To assist you in bringing clarity to your self-neglect patterns, let's unpack the negative influence your self-absorbed parents had that led you to default to self-neglect and reflexively put others first.

You Must Be Useful

Toxic parents value you only for your usefulness to them. When you make yourself useful, your parents consider you to be respectful. This kind of parenting conditions you to live a pattern of making yourself "useful" as a method of securing "love." By instinct, you learn to prioritize others and neglect yourself.

Remedy: Give yourself permission to stop catering to your parents' unreasonable requests for your time and attention. Your parents are used to getting their way and will certainly take notice as you step back and say no more often. If halting meeting their needs all at once feels like it will have too big of a consequence, step back a little at a time, by doing less for them in small increments, until you're brave enough to say no whenever you need to. In either case, you will face the unpleasant reaction that has kept you a prisoner to self-neglect. As hard as it is, find the willpower not to collapse under their negative manipulative influence and stay your course.

You Must Please Others

Pleasing implies cowering, becoming the lesser person in the relationship, posing no threat or challenge. It is a defense whereby you preemptively appease your parents by telling them what they want to hear, overexaggerating your affection for them, and seeking their acceptance though servile flattery. Over time, the pleasing response becomes a conditioned pattern of survival. Many survivors of emotionally abusive parents carry this self-neglecting behavioral pattern into their adult relationships.

To recognize people-pleasing behavior, consider whether you do the following:

- look to others to determine how you should feel or respond in a relationship or situation
- freeze up when trying to identify your feelings
- feel like you have no solid identity
- instinctually placate an unhappy person at the first sign of conflict

- recognize that you ignore your own beliefs, thoughts, and truths and accept those of the people around you to "keep the peace"

- experience unusual emotional responses toward people and things not directly or closely involved in your life, such as emotional outbursts at strangers or sudden feelings of unexpected sadness or worry throughout the day

- struggle to say no

- feel overwhelmed but continue to take on more responsibility if asked

- lack boundaries and are often taken advantage of in relationships

- feel uncomfortable or threatened when asked to give an opinion

- agree with everyone externally

- falsely assume you are at fault for another person's negative feelings

- overapologize

- feel resentful over things you have agreed to do

- feel angry at yourself and guilty most of the time

- feel excessive worry over the idea of someone being mad at you

- act like a chameleon by becoming like those around you in style, speech, and cadence

- have excessive needs for validation

- avoid conflict

- have great difficulty confronting people who hurt your feelings

Moment of truth: Pleasing through self-sacrifice is not a sustainable way to show others love.

Remedy: One way to stop people-pleasing is to practice facing conflict. Handling conflict is a skill set that can be learned. When in conflict, it is key to remember that you have the right to be the person you really are, that powerful person in your head who has always internally stood up to your parents at each emotional assault. When learning to handle conflict, let go of a desired outcome. Simply say what you need to say. This may be hard at first but will become easier with practice. Confidence is not developed by getting your way in a conflict. Confidence is developed through the facing of conflict. If your parents do not accept your boundaries, that is not your loss or your problem. As an adult, you are in the position to set any boundaries you need, and you should do so. It's called self-love.

Moment of truth: The way your parents have manipulated and abused you doesn't result in the desire to have a close, connected relationship with them.

You Must Have Low Self-Worth

Psychologically abusive parents understand that the lower your self-worth is, the easier you are to influence. If you do not believe you are worthy, you will seek finding your worth in other ways. Toxic parents find children who have a strong sense of self to be disrespectful. In fact, many of you have exhausted yourselves trying to reason or justify why your parents have done the horrible and spiteful things they have done. You can't find an answer because deep inside you are haunted by the question: Shouldn't your parents have been the people who treated you the most humanely? Unfortunately, you will find a plethora of instances of your abuse but be left without answers to make sense of why it happened. You surmise that you must be the problem, questioning yourself on how you could be better and do better.

Remedy: The biggest downfall that keeps you stuck in unsafe, one-sided relationships is fear. Fear forces you to put your own wants and needs, which would build your self-worth, on the back burner and prioritize those of others, like you have with your parents. To change this, you must decide that enough is enough and take on the role of being the person who champions for your rights by upholding the boundaries you set.

You Overcompensate

When you are made to feel that you are not enough, you overcompensate by making your life a series of experiences designed around everyone else, namely your parents. Following are signs you may be overcompensating.

You Overshare

Most of you overshare out of nervousness. The nervousness comes from a deep desire to "fill the space"—the emptiness and the awkwardness—between yourself and your parents. Because there is no love brought into the relationship, the space between yourself and your parents is vacuous. You want them to feel you respect them but can't seem to achieve that when their lines keep moving. Not knowing what will happen next causes you to overshare or overexplain to fill the space and feel closer to them. For example, a woman as a young girl had written letters to her parents, one for each, that read: "Do you love me? I know you do." In this letter, she couldn't bear to wait for their answer of whether they loved her or not, so she filled the space with the answer she needed to hear. The rest of each letter was filled with dialogue trying to prove to her parents that she was a good girl, worthy of their love and respect. She was desperately seeking their validation, which she never received. As an adult, this woman becomes furious at herself because she feels she talks too much in conversations when she doesn't need to. Through her healing journey, she has been able to uncover that her oversharing stems from the old feelings of nervousness she had as child, which led her to fill the space between herself and her parents to garner some feeling of agency over the direction of the relationship.

Remedy: When you feel the need to "fill the space," practice holding on to yourself by not allowing yourself to take over directing the conversation. Focus more on listening than on sharing.

You Overdo

The need for acceptance drives overdoing. You feel compelled, even obsessed with, trying not to burden others. This drive to overdo can put you in a position to be taken advantage of.

Remedy: Practice coasting a little more gently through life. Remind yourself that not everything needs to get done today, nor should you be held to anyone else's standard to make things right or perfect for them in their own life. You deserve rest and peace. You also deserve reciprocity.

You Try to Predict Next Steps in a Relationship

Because trust was not fundamental to your upbringing, you can become hypervigilant trying to predict all the next steps in a relationship in an attempt to establish a sense of psychological safety and to quell your worries and anxieties.

Remedy: Practice slowing down and trusting yourself. Everything you need to know about any person or situation will reveal itself in time. It is in you to make the right decisions for your life. Sometimes, in hindsight, you would have made a different decision, but that's okay.

You Perform to Win Love

Most of you had parents who demanded you perform to unreasonable standards to win their love and respect. Performance isn't love. Performance is a measurement of pass or fail. This type of parenting makes both love and respect conditional. You can perform your life away, fully neglect yourself, and still not win parental approval.

Remedy: Remind yourself that when someone loves you, you should not be placed in a position to continually earn their love. Those who love you would never require you neglect yourself to make them feel important.

You Feel Guilty for Having Needs of Your Own

Maladaptive guilt, discussed earlier, causes you to feel bad when you need to ask for something or when someone does something generous for you. After someone positively contributes to your life, you may find yourself apologizing for the effort they had to make to do this. It may not feel safe to accept anything from others for fear that you may be manipulated with a demand of owing them something in return.

Remedy: When someone does something nice for you, practice saying "thank you" in place of "You didn't have to do this. I feel bad." Remind yourself that you are worthy and that healthy people contribute to your life because they love seeing you happy.

You Justify When Things Go Wrong

You have been programmed to feel at fault when anything goes wrong, even though you have not done anything wrong. When faced with conflict, it is common to feel jumpy inside, triggering you to justify and explain your position to protect yourself from erroneous fault being directed toward you.

Remedy: Before reacting to justify your position, learn to take a minute. Take some deep breaths. Gather yourself. Your brain needs oxygen to think clearly. Process and gather the specifics around your part in any given situation to determine your role, if you had any. Remind yourself that all conversations can wait until you feel clear enough to communicate.

> **Moment of truth:** One of the most loving things you can do for yourself is to sit with the discomfort of letting other people be responsible for themselves.

As you have been learning, the easiest emotion to manipulate is fear. Fear makes you behave in certain ways, but it doesn't make you brave. When you are afraid of or cannot count on your parents, your spirit weakens, and you become a shell of the person you were born to be. This happens because your only choice to survive was to neglect your own needs to meet the needs of your parents.

Symptoms of Toxic Parent Abuse Victim Syndrome

Fearing your parents results in what I call *toxic parent abuse victim syndrome*. This syndrome is driven by the conditioned self-neglecting mindsets that you were forced to adopt as avenues for "respecting" your parents. A syndrome is a group of symptoms that occur together with consistency and are expressed through one's thoughts, emotions, and behaviors. The mindsets above are ingrained enough to become a syndrome of self-neglect. Let's explore the following symptoms of toxic parent abuse victim syndrome.

Fear That No One Will Believe You

Because most parents seem healthy from the outside, it feels pointless to try and get anyone to believe how malicious and vindictive they are behind closed doors. Emotional abuse can be so subtle that when it happens, others fail to recognize that what is being said or done is abuse. In the moment the abuse is happening, you might not even fully understand what is going on. All you know is that you suddenly feel consumed with feelings of intense confusion, upset, or humiliation for something your parents just publicly exposed.

One of your deepest hopes is that your friends and loved ones would recognize this as humiliating and stand up for you. Unfortunately, this rarely happens. Your loved ones most often doubt your claims of emotional abuse, take the side of your parents, and lean into the myth that all parents are good by dismissing your abuse with microaggressions, for example, by saying, "You must have misunderstood" and "Your parents would never intentionally hurt you." This lack of belief coming from others doubles the dose of your damage. Not only does it fracture your faith in the people you love, but more importantly it also leads you to question yourself on whether the abuse you experienced took place or not. You think to yourself, *Maybe I did read too much into their words or imagined that look of disgust on their face or tone in their voice.* You didn't.

Terror of the Gossip Train

Your parents use gossip to twist the facts about your supposed out-of-control, disrespectful, unstable behavior to discredit your truth. Why do they do this? The answer is simple: People inherently believe parents over children. People also tend to believe a story corroborated by more than one person. Even worse, when you react to the gossip being spread, people use your desperate need to right the wrong as evidence of your lack of respect for your parents.

Fear of Being Cast Out

When your parents, family, friends, and intimate partners refuse to believe you, it makes you feel like you do not exist. This is exactly what your parents need to isolate you even further. A great example is when Britney Spears told a judge that when this judge didn't believe the story of her abuse, she felt dead, like she didn't matter. Of course, Spears's father claimed he had only her best interest at heart. What your toxic parents know is that you are more likely to doubt your perceptions of their abuse when you cannot turn to anyone for support to validate your side of the story. You may even have friends or partners who further discount your experience by encouraging you to make amends with your parents. For example, people will tell you, "Your parents are getting older and frailer," and warn you that setting boundaries with your parents will be a mistake you will later regret. This fear drives many of you to hang on to the unhealthy relationship you have with them out of fear of being misunderstood and ostracized by others, rather than for any desire to maintain a close connection to your parents.

Trouble Confronting

You have learned that confronting your parents doesn't work, nor does escaping your situation, so you freeze under the pressures of others. You hold back on creating the emotional distance you need from your parents to protect yourself for fear of seeming disrespectful.

Difficulty Making Decisions

When parents bully you, the bullying often involves frequent implications that you make bad decisions and can't do anything right. Over time, you absorb these insults and attach them to your self-perception. This causes you to constantly second-guess yourself.

Consistent Worry You Have Done Something Wrong

Your parents avoid accountability for their abuse through deceit. If you dare to stand up for yourself, they react with disgust and say things such as "How dare you question me!" These bombardments of manipulation leave you feeling helpless, dependent, and often grateful your parents are even willing to be around you, considering how awful you are. Even after creating distance or severing ties, you will likely carry forward the belief that you can't do anything right and may struggle to accept that you didn't cause those problems.

Unexplained Physical Symptoms

The psyche can handle only so much internalized stress before it externalizes its symptoms into the physical body. Those symptoms include but are not limited to changes in appetite, stomach upset, insomnia, body aches, fatigue, chronic headaches, asthma, sore throat, and allergies.

Belief You Have No Real Identity

The changes you make in yourself to appease your parents lead to the loss of the development of a strong sense of self. Without a strong sense of who you are, it can prove difficult to truly enjoy life. Initiating actions toward the things you desire is often lost to fear and procrastination, making you feel hollow and stagnant.

Anxiety and Depression

The significant stress you face from the two most important and influential people in your life can trigger unremitting feelings of anxiety and depression, including sadness and hopelessness. This hopelessness is powerful enough to cause you to lose interest in things that used to bring you peace, making it a struggle to see any promising outcomes for your future.

Healing from Toxic Parent Abuse Victim Syndrome

The symptoms of toxic parent abuse victim syndrome are real. These are symptoms survivors can suffer in some way nearly every day of their life. It is hard to view yourself as worthy or powerful under these conditions. However, just because this syndrome is real does not mean you cannot rise from the ashes of the hell you were raised in. You absolutely can. Let's look at strategies to help you do this.

Allow me to assure you that it is possible to move away from being the victim of your abusive and manipulative parents into the strong leader of your own life. The abuse enlivens a spirit in you that wants to fight against them. You must be persistent in the act of reminding yourself of your truth—to believe and stand on the words your parents refuse to hear. To back this movement, there must be a strong internal desire to be genuinely happy and live your life as you envision yourself living it. You have every right to separate, individuate, and establish your own empowered, resilient identity. This is not a betrayal of your parents, but rather an organic and necessary step in your development. The following actions will help you heal from toxic parent abuse victim syndrome.

Define Your Lines of Tolerance

You will know where your lines of tolerance are by how you feel. Pay close attention to feelings of discomfort, anger, or resentment when someone does something you don't like. These are the whispers that something is off, and boundaries need to be set.

Set Boundaries

Boundaries are the conversations or silent actions you take to protect your lines of tolerance. Boundaries can be both spoken and unspoken. Boundaries can be set in a variety of ways: You can confront directly, state what your need is, and refuse to engage further. You can send a handwritten note via mail, email, or text communicating what boundary you are setting. You can use your feet to silently distance yourself from anyone who is mistreating you, no explanation needed. You have every right to protect your feelings and personal space.

It's easy to get stuck in the frustration of knowing that your parents do not or will not care if you set boundaries with them. There is a natural and deep sadness inside knowing that they will not take accountability for what they have done to get you to this point. You're right. If your parents didn't care or take accountability while in a relationship with you, they certainly will not care to take accountability out of a relationship with you. Therefore, if you are setting boundaries out of the hope that it will provoke your parents into caring and taking accountability, you are not setting boundaries for the right reasons. You are setting boundaries to try and change your parents, to get them to wake up. They won't.

Moment of truth: At your lines of tolerance, silence is your superpower.

Setting boundaries with character disordered parents is much different than setting limits with healthy parents. Too often, the way the literature teaches setting boundaries gives the false impression that if you set a boundary with someone that you will establish control over that person's undesirable behavior in your life. In a healthy relationship, that may be so. However, in a toxic relationship, setting boundaries from this mindset doesn't work. Emotionally abusive and manipulative parents will not give you the accountability or remorse you are looking for. When you set boundaries with your parents, they use this information to become even more acutely aware of where and how they have successfully hurt you and where and how they can continue to do so. They willfully cross the exact boundaries you set to show you that you have no power. In their minds, they are your parents and therefore entitled to do what they please to you. Boundaries with toxic parents must be based in self-control, rather than on any control over another. You must demonstrate self-control by not engaging when they deliberately cross your lines. If your parents can provoke you into an emotional reaction about your stated limits, they have you right where they want you. This places them at the center of your attention, with you in the disempowered position feeling frustrated and hurt. Pleading with them to see the negative results of their flagrant, abusive behaviors gives them even more attention. They love this. This is the kind of fuel they crave, disempowering you.

Seek Support

The hard work of life doesn't have to be accomplished alone. This may be how you had to survive your childhood, but as an adult, you have the choice to reach for help and support from many sources, including a therapist, a group, an online outlet, a book, a friend, a pet, an intimate partner, or all of the above. The more support you have, the more empowered you become.

Live Your Own Life

You have a right to live your life. It's your life to live. You are smart, capable, and a hell of a lot more worthy than being an emotional underling to toxic parents. The less space your abusive and manipulative parents take up in your life, the more fully and passionately you give yourself the opportunity to exit.

Distance Yourself from Those Who Support Your Parents

Anyone who pressures and guilts you for taking steps away from your emotionally abusive parents is not a person who will see you, understand, or genuinely support you. They may accept your decision under their own negative judgment, but this also means you will likely encounter that negativity each time you're around them. You cannot live your best life tethered to the ignorant judgments of others.

Envision and Live Your Own Life

You have permission to live a full life. What kind of life do you want to see for yourself? What are your goals and desires? Write them down. Sit quietly for a few minutes and say each thing you would like to happen out loud, envisioning those things as being on their way to you right now. Practice this as often as you can.

Define Yourself

Examining the toxicity of your parents helps you define yourself as different from them. It helps you see that you were not and are not the source of their happiness or unhappiness. You are not their problem. They are their own problem. This difference in definition between yourself and them, healthy versus unhealthy, is what sets you on the course for seeing yourself correctly and developing the self-respect you deserve to have and feel. Again, when parents are unhealthy, you are taught that to respect your parents, you must neglect yourself. To be considered respectful, they must always come first and you last.

This is not love.

CHAPTER 7

What Love Based in Respect Feels Like

Love is a fascinating thing. Love can regenerate over and over. It takes a tremendous amount of trauma to squash the love a child feels for their parent. Even if you have established distance or no contact with your parents, it does not mean you do not love them. Most often you do love them.

You have created emotional distance or established no contact because they have lost your respect. Respect, unlike love, can be lost, and it can be lost forever. When respect is lost, so is trust. When trust is lost, so is the value and stability of that relationship. When you lose respect for your parents, it causes you to no longer like them as people. When you don't like people, including your parents, you don't want to be around them. You don't respect your parents because their parenting has exposed the deceitfulness, immaturity, and self-centeredness of their character.

I, and most of you, do not wish our parents any ill will when creating distance or establishing definitive boundaries between ourselves and them. However, what we survivors of emotionally abusive parents do know is that we simply cannot have that type of betrayal, abuse, and manipulation in our life and still be mentally and emotionally well. Your parents have proven, time and again, that spending time around them is nothing short of an emotionally draining, horrific experience.

Moment of truth: Surviving a lifetime of parental manipulation and abuse is a violent, emotional roller-coaster ride that never slows down enough for you to get off safely. Eventually, you will have to jump.

Love and Respect Require Emotional Safety

Emotional safety is a psychological state of feeling protected from harm or other undesirable outcomes. A feeling of well-being cannot happen if you do not first feel safe. Psychologically abusive parents do not provide emotional safety. This is different from the physical security your home may have provided growing up. Having physical security means you have a place to live and grow up. When you live in an environment of emotional abuse and manipulation, the inside of that environment is not safe. Your "home" is a place of confinement. You are forced to live in conditions that make you too nervous to relax for fear you may miss something or accidentally do something that threatens your current or future security.

Some of the most damaging abuse is emotional, where there appears to be no real pattern, rhyme, or reason for a parent's sudden 180-degree turn away from you after a time of great affection. This is incredibly destabilizing. Emotional abuse may not be identifiable by physical markers. However, this type of abuse is potent enough to break the hearts and spirits of children—leaving you to function with an intense and gripping tightness in your chest. Your heart aches and races because you have no control over your daily existence. There is always some new emotional game you are forced to play: Perhaps it is another divorce, another bad mood, another day of being ostracized or punished for no valid reason, another day feeling like you amount to nothing more than a burden to your parents' life that they resent sacrificing for, or another day of being shamed, yelled at, and criticized for not meeting the selfish needs of your parents. Trying to make any meaningful progress with a parent like this is like trying to nail Jell-O to a wall. When this is your normal, it makes looking forward to new things dreadful rather than hopeful. This is because you have been trained to look for what is scary or wrong in the new things that are coming in order to prepare and protect yourself from further or unknown hurts.

Sadly, once you are out of childhood, these maladaptive reactions remain easily triggered by feelings of uncertainty. In many situations, you automatically default to fear. Because you have experienced a lifetime of emotional trauma, it is difficult to imagine that things in life could go well for you. You have been conditioned to live from such deep levels of stress that it is nearly impossible to ease into the natural flow of life. You nervously believe that if you are not consistently working to prove your worth that something or someone meaningful will be taken from you. Too many of us, myself included, have extreme trouble learning to calm down because we don't know how to trust. This is what trauma does. This is how dysfunctional parents rob you of the sweetness life has to offer. It is your life's work to learn a new way of living through trusting yourself rather than others.

How to Create Feelings of Psychological Safety

Here are some ways you can help create feelings of psychological safety in your life.

Awareness

Intentionally bring awareness to how you feel. If you feel unsafe, afraid, or nervous, accept these feelings for what they are. Let go of trying to convince yourself that what you are feeling is unwarranted, crazy, or wrong. You are not crazy. Open your heart to your emotions and validate them. Start with a current emotion and work backward to the situation or person that triggered it. You were triggered for a reason. Try to identify that reason. This will help you define where your boundaries need to be.

Reassurance

When you feel unsafe, seek reassurance, rather than trying to suppress this feeling. For example, a compassionate human voice or the privacy of prayer, a journal, or meditation may prove calming and clarifying.

Friend Trick

If your friend were coming to you with your exact triggering circumstances and feelings, how would you advise them to take care of themselves? Your next step is to take the lead and follow your own advice.

Mindfulness

Stay connected to the moment and remind yourself that you're no longer trapped in your childhood where you had no power over your circumstances. As an adult, you have power.

Relationship Break

If you have made poor relationship decisions, take a break from relationships to focus on yourself for a while.

Follow-Through

Egocentric parents are noncommittal and inconsistent. Following through *for* yourself *to* yourself is a solid way to soothe the wound of broken promises. For example, practice saying no when you need to say no, and yes when you need to say yes. You are worthy of follow-through.

Me Time

Take time to rest in your own company. This is not being selfish. It's essential for self-care.

Practice

Practicing this type of healing work will create a solid feeling of psychological safety you can rely on when needed. Once inner safety is operating well, you start trusting yourself to make bigger and better decisions. As you make bigger life-enhancing decisions, you also start making healthier decisions in love and relationships. When you trust yourself, it leads you to love yourself more deeply. When you love yourself, people naturally find you more lovable.

Love Based in Respect Creates Feelings of Well-Being

Mistreatment couched as parenting is horrific and confusing enough to deeply damage your belief in humanity. If you were emotionally abused, your parents' approach to love wasn't love. It was manipulation. Regardless, because you craved their love, you worked hard to love them despite all the pain they caused you. Why? Because your survival was dependent upon this love and commitment from you. This is extremely confusing to work through as you begin to heal. Yet, it must be examined because, unfortunately, you have learned to love and depend on those who knowingly did things to damage you. The habit of loving abusers often proves hard to break.

> **Moment of truth:** When you genuinely love someone, you cannot abuse them. You wouldn't be able to fathom it.

For example, a woman shared that her mother had finally pushed her abuses too far, and this woman had had enough. This woman took it upon herself to start standing up to her mother's manipulations, causing her mother to banish this woman from her life. This mother swiftly coerced this woman's two sisters to turn against her. To this day, this woman wonders why and how something like this could happen. She shared she has lost many years of her life drowning in feelings of intense grief because she could not find a way to wrap her head around how setting these types of boundaries on her mother would lead to this result. That her mother loved her so little was a reality that shook this woman to her core. The boundaries this woman set were healthy.

A healing way to look at these horrible circumstances with your parents is to remember that love and abuse cannot healthfully coexist. You must promote the part of yourself that believes you are allowed to liberate yourself from this dysfunctional pattern of seeing the parents who abused you as people worthy of your love. Stepping back from your parents requires blind faith.

Step Back and Stand Your Ground

You have enough experience to know that if you speak up for yourself, the conflict with your parents is rarely worth the cost. Your parents have shown they could care less if you rage, cry, or plead with them to reason with you. The gift of stepping back is that it allows you to see the whole picture. You can recognize that your parents' refusal to hear what you have to say is essentially a boundary they are setting with you. When your parents make their lack of interest in hearing your perception of events obvious, your silence directly respects their stated boundary of not wanting to hear you. Bizarrely, toxic parents also cannot stand your silence, the silence in you they demand, when it is given to them. Not your issue. They can't have it both ways.

You must find the courage to stand your solid ground and not allow yourself to sink further into the emotional quicksand of their twisted nonsense. You must access that part of you that knows without any doubt that how you are being treated is wrong. With genuine love, there are no games. There are no applications of guilt or obligation used to keep you stuck. Love is about freedom. Abuse is about subjugation. You must possess the wisdom to know the difference.

Simple steps to standing your solid ground include the following.

- Step back and allow for distance and silence.

- When confronted on your silence, state that your silence is respectful of your parents' lack of openness to listen to what you have say.

- If provoked into conflict, state clearly you will not engage further.

- End the conversation by saying you will agree to disagree (whether they do or not).

Healthy Choices

You have the right to make choices supportive of your psychological health and well-being. This will mean setting clear boundaries, maybe even eliminating contact, with your parents. These boundaries often need to include the halfway people who give your parents access to you. I covered this topic in my book *Adult Survivors of Toxic Family Members* (Campbell 2022). You cannot live with joy and fulfillment surrounded by poisonous people and circumstances. Your happiness is not outside of you, but inside. Therefore, the choices you make must be centered on taking agency over your inner world. The truth is: You know deep down when you are unhappy. You know when you are being abused and manipulated. You know when you are being lied to, betrayed, and taken advantage of. You know when things in your life need to change. The reality of this knowing, however, is frightening.

Fear is powerful enough to get you to betray what you know. When you feel fear, it is easier to go against what you know by questioning its validity than to accept the painful truths beneath the surface. Avoidance has no doubt led many of you to fill your life with distractions and different forms of denial, and to try to convince yourself that things in your life are better than they are. Loving yourself means facing your harsher realities and acting upon them in the spirit of standing firmly behind who you are and what you need, want, and deserve to live, feel, and experience. It is important to challenge the way you think about things when you are in fear. When you are in fear, you are out of alignment with your power. Instead, lean toward viewing things from a higher level of consciousness and seeing that not all things that feel like a loss are truly a loss. Consider that they may rather be a gain.

Moment of truth: Loving the wrong people results in living an incredibly unhappy life.

Not All Things That Feel like a Loss Are a Loss

Consider that what seems like a loss could instead be a gain. To help develop the mindset for believing that not all things that feel like a loss are a loss, try the following strategies.

Listen to Yourself

Your parents have proven they are not interested in hearing your version of things. When you accept that they will not hear you, you can turn your focus to listening, trusting, and validating your own experience of them. This will help you move on. This is a gain.

Embrace the Unknown

It takes far greater courage to let go and lean toward the unknown than it does to clutch and hang on to what is familiar and no longer serving you. You don't have to remain committed to emotionally imprisoning parents. You can set boundaries. Life will go on. You will be okay. This is a gain.

Let Go

You can teach your heart that some things, including a relationship with your parents, aren't always meant to last forever. Your parents have taught you important lessons about what love is not, which helps you better define what love is. This is a gain.

Be Your Own Advocate

When you drop the fear-based attachment to your emotionally abusive parents, your soul becomes lighter. You feel the loss, but that loss can be replaced with feelings of acceptance. You can become your own advocate. This is a gain.

Bolster Your Self-Esteem

The biggest part of yourself that you lose in creating distance from your emotionally abusive parents is the person they have made you become, a person with low self-esteem. When you set yourself free from the lowly person they defined you as, your self-esteem stands to increase. This is a gain.

Relish Being Alone

Time and distance from the parents who emotionally manipulate you unearths that all the truths you knew deep inside about them are, in fact, real. Being alone illuminates a clarity you could never have gained in the confusion and chaos of being in a close relationship with them. This is a gain.

Cut Off Relationships

When you empower yourself to let go of the parents who have mis-treated you, this empowers you to also let go of all of those who have stood complicit to your abuse. This is a gain.

Move Toward Self-Respect

You are stronger than you think. You may not feel that right now, but the next chapter will open a discussion on the development of self-respect. Once you understand how fear became your default emotion, you have the potential to gain the wisdom and traction necessary to transform your relationship with yourself to be more kind, compassionate, and considerate. Yes, you deserve to be treated with consideration, heard, and taken seriously.

> **Moment of truth:** When you have self-respect, your addiction to joy grows stronger than any addiction to fear you learned to have.

CHAPTER 8

Respecting Yourself

Self-respect is a confusing topic for survivors of parental emotional abuse. When you have never experienced being respected by your parents, it is hard to grasp that you, on your own, could hold yourself in high esteem and believe that you are worthy of being treated well. It holds true that when your parents do not respect you, you learn not to respect yourself. It is difficult to imagine setting boundaries with others and not tolerating their poor treatment when you have been fed a steady diet of all these things growing up without any refuting evidence. It is difficult to raise self-esteem when you have no esteem to start from. However, you are not doomed unless you do not try.

> **Moment of truth:** Your idea of love is largely determined by how your parents love you.

Developing Self-Respect

The greatest thing about respect is that respect is learned. Your abusive and manipulative parents modeled everything that the value of true respect is not. Respect has nothing to do with demands or threats around behavior or obedience. Respect starts with love and a concern for how someone feels about you in their heart, which shows itself in how they treat you. To start developing healthy self-respect, start treating yourself in the following ways.

Be Nice to Yourself

The voice in your head is often the deadliest of all. You learned to talk to (emotionally abuse) yourself in the same ways your parents did.

Remedy: Be kind, fair, and civil to yourself. Talk to yourself in the same tone and with the same love that you would offer your own children, best friend, pet, or colleague.

Be Yourself

Now that you are not under the direct control of your parents, you have the freedom to be the person you always wanted to be but were blocked from actualizing.

Remedy: Envision who the free, unencumbered person is who is inside of you. Write down those traits, such as free-spirited, confident, discerning, and fair. Commit to living one trait per day, thereby establishing these traits as your new healthy habits and behavioral patterns.

Get Moving

Fear, anxiety, and depression can lead to a life of inaction. The more inaction there is in your life, the deeper the dive you take into negative mood states.

Remedy: Movement is medicine. Movement stimulates the chemicals in the brain that activate positive mood and outlook. Start walking, gardening, doing yoga, exercising, dancing, or doing anything that gets you moving and see how drastically your life will improve.

Find Joy in Imperfection

Toxic parents make you feel useless, difficult, pathetic, and unwanted, as well as a waste of their time. Your worth is always at risk of not being enough. This is a lie.

Remedy: It is imperative you stop reflexively telling yourself this lie: "If you're not acting, being, or performing to perfection, you have little value." Your parents demanding perfection from you, when they themselves were far from perfect, makes no sense. Pressuring yourself to be perfect is equally nonsensical. No one is perfect, and that is a beautiful thing. Did you know that the further from perfect others perceive you to be, the more approachable you become? Find the joys in your imperfections. These imperfections, when managed with love and a sense of humor, are likely the most precious parts of your personality.

Learn from Mistakes

Toxic parents raise you to believe that any slip in perfection coming from you was fatal and deserving of their chastisement.

Remedy: Mistakes are not fatal. Temper your thoughts and assumptions around the worst-case scenarios your mind makes up. Own your experiences by changing the behavior that led you to make whatever human mistake you made and move forward lesson in hand.

Focus on What You Can Change

When your parents made a primary focus of your relationship pointing out the smallest idiosyncrasies of your personality, it is hard to believe there is a viable way to change yourself. Instead, you likely feel consumed with worry as you incessantly overanalyze the shortcomings you have been systematically trained to focus on.

Remedy: Many of your resilient traits that were rejected by your parents, such as standing up for yourself or telling the truth, are gifts of strength you possess and can utilize going forward. You cannot change your parents, but you can change yourself and what you will and will not make space for in your life.

Consider Yourself

You grew up not being considered and believing you were not deserving of your parents' time, consideration, or compassion.

Remedy: You have permission to consider yourself—to consider what is right and wrong for you. You have the right to nurture and act on things of personal importance and honor how you feel. Your voice, your choice.

Nurture Positive Relationships

If you are surrounded by and drowning in toxic relationships of all kinds, you will continue to replicate the familiarity of the mistreatment your parents raised you in, placing you back in fear and disempowerment.

Remedy: You get to choose the company you keep as an adult. Choose wisely.

Create a New Narrative

When you take it upon yourself to master these new skills, you will develop a true sense of your personal value and significance. This type of transformation helps you shift out of the chaos-and-drama paradigm into a more peaceful and unencumbered existence. This type of work is worthy work. It is your right to protect the positive changes you are making from the parents and other involved family members or friends who desire to keep you stuck in the negative narrative of you they are most comfortable with. It is your right to create a new narrative, one in which you flourish.

Protect Your Peace

Protecting your peace is about self-care. It is about your personal rights to take time for this type of activity. Protecting your peace requires mindfulness and self-awareness. It requires the commitment to no longer afford your parents the opportunity to highjack your emotional stability from underneath you via their own selfish demands, making you feel obligated toward them. The limits you set to protect your peace must be stronger than your soft heart. Hold steadfast to your lines. Remind yourself that the limits you are setting to protect your peace are normal, healthy, and necessary.

> **Moment of truth:** If you set limits loosely, your parents will not take you or your limits seriously.

When you start protecting your peace, expect that the following may happen.

- Your emotionally abusive parents will vehemently resist losing access to the parts of you they once had control over. Set your limits anyway. If they keep pushing, they may force you to push them out of your life by virtue of their own inability to be respectful of your stated needs.

- Setting limits or creating distance between yourself and your parents does not make you a bad person, a bad child, or a bad family member. Remember, emotionally abusive parents see you as bad whether you set limits or not, so no need to allow your fears to factor in when making self-care decisions.

- You have no control over the unwarranted blame your parents cast your way. What you do have control over is protecting yourself, and if doing this makes you a "bad guy," then so be it. For example, a woman shared that she could not stand how enmeshing and demanding her mother was in every area of her life. Any boundaries she set were deemed cruel and anti-family by her mother. To get her way, this mother enlisted several of her friends to contact my patient with the task of setting her straight on her poor treatment of her mother "who has always done so much for her children." These enlisted allies were condescending and punitive toward this woman. They had no business involving themselves in the relationship between her and her mother. When confronted, this mother would say, "I have no control over whether my friends decide to call my daughter." This lack of consideration was hurtful to this woman who was asking for nothing more than basic respect from her egocentric mother. The only selfish person in that dynamic was the mother.

- No matter what happens, stand firm in protecting your peace. It is your right.

- Silence is often the best way to say everything your words can't.

None of us wants to be placed in a position with our parents where we must sacrifice our personal rights toward greater independence and separation to maintain our relationships with them. Something as healthy as independence should not be a bargaining chip when you are old enough to support yourself. Being independent is what is developmentally and socially appropriate. It is confusing that when you grow to embrace the independence your parents forced on you as a threat while you were under their control, you are suddenly deemed antifamily when you are old enough to embrace it. Let me assure you that you are not a bad person for wanting to escape the clutches of immature, selfish, controlling parents to have a chance at creating and living your best life. If they brand you as bad for doing this, then that is their opinion.

All Children Want to Be Good

The desire to be seen as good in the eyes of your parents is natural. This is true even in the tragic story of Gabriel Fernandez, who died from the injuries he sustained under the abuse of his mother and her boyfriend. All Gabriel wanted was to be seen as good in his mother's eyes. His last school project, before he was murdered, was a sheet to fill out for his mother on Valentine's Day, where he wrote down that the gift he wanted to give his mother was to "be good" so she would love him. He was murdered just a few weeks later. The desire to be loved, supported, and accepted by your parents is profound enough to have you shape-shifting your personality to get even a small taste of their love.

Emotionally abusive and manipulative parents set the stage for your *unworthiness* from the very beginning of your life. From fear, you start rushing. You rush to please. You rush to make others happy, and you rush your healing by skipping your grieving to try and get a taste of love from the emotionally unavailable parents who raised you. You do this because you want and need the love and approval of your parents to one day confidently and freely spread your own wings. At some point, you run out of the energy to keep trying to be good enough for them. Enough finally becomes enough. This is a healthy place to be because it aligns with reality. Knowing when enough is enough is a pivotal turning point.

Reaching a Turning Point

As an adult, you have the authority to define the roles you choose to play in your life and the roles other people will play in it. As a child, you had no choice in the role you were cast in by your parents. If you wanted to survive, you had to take the role you were given, even if being in that role was completely abusive and unfair. Once you are able, it is your right to captain your own ship and create the life you have always wanted to live. You will learn in the next chapter what your given role in your family system was and how to shift from that given role into your chosen role in this world, even when that means creating separation between yourself and your parents.

CHAPTER 9

Your Role in the
Family System

There is no easy way out of a psychologically abusive family because you're not allowed to go peacefully, as hard as you may try. Wanting separation from severely character disordered parents has all the same elements of leaving a cult. In a cult, there are elders or people in authority. These power-holders determine the pecking order of all other members. You are assigned your role without choice. Your role can change only if those in power make that change. Under abusive and manipulative parents, children hold the lowest ranking. You have no freedom, and you never will. The difference between a family and a cult is that people choose to be part of a cult (unless they are born into it), while children don't choose to be part of their family.

The similarities between cults and toxic families include the following.

- There is an unquestioning adherence to the power-holders, dead or alive.

- Doubts and questions about the morality or functionality of the group are discouraged and punished.

- The power-holders oversee everyone's destiny. They attempt to control how you think, feel, and behave. Their realm of control extends to decisions such as how you dress, where you live, how you get educated, and whom you marry.

- You are indoctrinated to hold the belief that the power-holders are all-knowing and rank as more important than all others in the group.

- There is an us-versus-them mentality. Power-holders ostracize, punish, and threaten anyone who is not in alignment with their values.

- The power-holders induce feelings of shame and guilt to gain influence and control over you. They use peer pressure and other subtle forms of persuasion based on threat.

- No one in the group (family) is allowed to veer from their assigned role. Everyone is systematically encouraged to end all contact with anyone outside the group (family).

- Group (family) members are indoctrinated to feel terrified of the resulting backlash to themselves or others if they leave, or even consider leaving, the group (family).

- If you attempt to create any distance from the group, the power-holders will incite a smear campaign to bully you into returning.

Under the rule of emotionally abusive and manipulative parents, having or expressing your authentic self was not condoned. You were not given unconditional love or the space to develop a healthy conscience. There was no flexibility, creativity, or fun, and you were robbed of your own free will. The only existence allowed was for you to uphold the false image of the goodness of your parents. What your parents said was law. If you did not follow along, you were guilted and shamed. You were shamed into a life of codependency and obedience. Living in a family like this is demoralizing.

Abuse of Power Is Abuse

Depending upon who holds the most power, there is a natural asymmetry of influence between a dominant parent and subservient parent, a parent and child, older to younger siblings, stronger to weaker siblings, and male to female siblings. Whatever the asymmetry is, it manifests as the abuse of unequal power, just as it does in a cult. Sadly, the misuse of power in family relationships is socially sanctioned and often seen as normal. This is not so in a cult. In a family, parents naturally have more power than children. This also means that children are too often trapped in families they cannot escape, with parents who use their more powerful position to exploit them and encourage all other family members to take part. Understanding the varying dynamics of unequal power set up by power-holding parents will help you see how the entire family system functions on dysfunction and which family member is the most likely to escape.

Assigned Roles in the Family System

Emotionally abusive and manipulative parents demand everyone play the roles assigned to them and wear whatever masks are required to present a filtered and rehearsed family image. Because there is such a pressure to make the family look good, a more passive parent and children will do their best to uphold the external image deemed important by the dominant parent. This type of control extinguishes natural spontaneous attitudes by the passive parent and children that could risk going against the rigid rules they are expected to adhere to. The passive parent and children are brainwashed to believe "No matter what happens at home, there are worse spouses and parents out there." The dominant parent expects their abuses to be regarded as normal and acceptable.

Let's take a look at pairings of different assigned family roles.

Authoritarian Parent, Subservient Parent

A typical pattern between toxic parents is one parent holds an emotionally superior position to the other. This authoritative parent is the person who runs the show and defines the roles of everyone in the family. The dominant parent is feared by all and enabled to be controlling and abusive by the subservient parent. The subservient parent is treated poorly and given little value unless this parent can be used to further the dominant parent's reign of terror. The subservient parent lives in fear, is conflict avoidant, and is complicit in the abuse of their children. A healthier, more self-confident parent would not allow their children to be abused under any circumstances, especially by their other parent. If necessary, the healthier parent would turn away from their spouse to protect their children. The subservient parent who fails to stand up to the authoritative parent is abusive to their children by proxy.

Authoritarian Parent, Bad (Subservient) Child

Parents who abuse their relative power over their children see themselves as above and their children as below. These parents have unrealistic expectations for respect, loyalty, and adoration from their children, yet give none in return. They will deceive, snoop, criticize, and manipulate, but children are expected to remain perfect. Otherwise, they will promptly be cast out. The child who is unable to keep hold of their anger and frustration is given the role of bad (subservient) child. The bad child is the one family member who rebels because they cannot tolerate the lack of fairness of the family system. Subsequently, the authoritative parent forces everyone in the family to turn against this child.

Your parent may have authority by age but too often not by maturity. The more abuse you tolerate, the more elastic you become in absorbing it. You become so worn down that you give in and begin to reason that you are responsible for changing because you are bad. Yet, you are stuck in the confusion and lack of justice of how your parent gets away with the exact behaviors you are being punished for. There is no justice for children raised under emotionally abusive parents.

You are forced into the below position for one primary reason: If you are bad, your parent doesn't have to acknowledge any feelings of guilt (conscious or not) for how they harm you. They hold the belief that being the parent excuses and justifies the harshness of their treatment. They want parent-fearing children. It is far more convenient for them to cast blame onto their children, who have no other choice but to take it. The easiest person for any adult to take advantage of is a child. Emotionally corrupt parents do this to a "bad child"—and also to a "good child." The goal of differential treatment is to pit siblings against each other. The more against each other siblings are, the more manipulative power the authoritative parent has over controlling both, and the less likely siblings are to come together and start a revolt.

Authoritarian (Good) Child, Bad (Subservient) Child

Emotionally abusive and manipulative parents use the divide-and-conquer method to weaken the emotional fortitude of their children and the bonds their children have with all other family members. For example, my parents tolerated me and took physical care of me, but I never got the feeling they were ever truly happy to see my face. This was not the case for my sibling. He had the experience of their joy and admiration for his impeccable performance in sports and school. But was that love? Love of his person? No, it wasn't. It was the love they felt when he did something to shine up the family image. He was and is required to keep that performance up. I was not outgoing or nearly as shiny and remained a recluse in my own family and to those in my social world. My sibling's natural extroverted social charm further cast me into a dark place, not because of him, but because of our assigned roles. Roles that neither of us chose. It has always baffled me that both my parents had married multiple times each and demonstrated many other obvious dysfunctions, all which was common knowledge, where any person should have been able to peek into my life and see how alone I was and have some understanding of my pain. Yet, no one could figure out why I wasn't thriving simply because my sibling seemingly was.

The perpetuated belief that all parents love their children caused outsiders to overlook my pain. Under the narrative that all parents are good and love their children, people misassumed that if my parents were really that bad, then both children would not be thriving. It depends upon how one defines thriving. Unseen to outsiders, including our parents, perhaps my sibling wasn't thriving at all, but was using areas of performance to escape his pain. I knew he wasn't thriving privately. He performed well under pressure. His performance made him look good, which gave him a public free pass. This remains so even when he has done and continues to do some of the most cruel and deceitful things to those he claims to love the most. His deceitful atrocities have been both enabled and encouraged by my parents and many others, serving to keep him under our parents' rule as a bargain for keeping his secrets. The enmeshment between my parents and sibling is truly tragic, especially for my sibling. My sibling, as the "good one," was under the direct care of our highly dysfunctional parents, sadly taking on their deceitful and abusive traits as his own, while I was left largely alone to take care of myself.

It genuinely saddens me that my sibling will have to meet his maker one day, where there will be no one there to enable, lie for, or justify his actions against the ugliest of truths he knows exist deep down. Today, I consider myself the lucky one. Sadly, it is typical of highly dysfunctional parents to put a halo on one child and demonize another. This isn't home. This is hell.

Golden (Authoritarian) Child

The golden child basks in their superior status. They love being close to and pleasing their godlike parents. The fear of being demoted motivates the golden child to perform to the best of their ability to maintain their superior position. They avoid any real contact with a so-called bad sibling to not catch the "loser kid" virus. They become as abusive to the bad child sibling as their parents are. The parents often encourage this abuse. The rules between these roles are lopsided. The golden child can misbehave, and this somehow serves to elevate this child's status to those in the mob who justify the golden child's horrible and selfish behavior. As this false story of the golden child's goodness continues, this child's ego grows, causing them to believe they can do no wrong. Manipulative parents excessively overvalue their golden child in exchange for the golden child's blind obedience.

In the most basic explanation of the golden child dynamic, it is common to see that as the golden child ages, they expect everyone in their life, including their spouse and kids, to give them the star treatment. This golden child suffers from "main character syndrome." There are no rules for golden children. If the golden child finds success in a career, they demand being the leader and often make those who work under them miserable. When golden children become parents, they demand perfection from their children. In tandem, they resent it if their children challenge their superior status in any way, including succeeding beyond them. To secure their position as the center of the universe, the golden child forces their children to be under their rule. Thus, the generational abuse often continues through the golden child.

I recognize there are children who were given the golden child role but did not feel like they were a golden child. These humbler golden children do not pass down nearly as much generational trauma to their own children. There are many variations of this dynamic that go beyond the scope of the general and most common dynamic I am explaining here. At the core, however, is siblings each having a different set of rules, which creates inequality. These differing levels of fairness lead to one sibling not liking the other. For example, one woman who was the golden child would hear her mother say to her older sister, "Too bad you're not as pretty as your sister" or "Don't you see how smart your little sister is? You should try and be more like her." This put the woman at the mercy of her older sister, who had such rage over always being compared to her that she would hold this woman down and spit on her face when they were growing up. The woman who was her mother's golden child became her sister's scapegoat. Today, as adults, the dynamic still has not changed. This woman's older sister emotionally abuses and smears this woman, even as this woman tries valiantly to please her and make peace to establish some type of healthy connection. The other siblings, too afraid to step in and help this woman with her sister, enable the sister's abuse. This woman is left out of all holidays and other family events, and her other siblings will see her only separately from her sister. Whoever the scapegoat is, over time, the person who is cast in this role and the others who contribute to it come to accept this abusive pattern as reasonable. In this scenario, the unhealed bad child passes on the generational trauma.

> **Moment of truth:** No matter whether you started as the golden child or were always the bad child, anyone who dares to leave the family will be moved into the scapegoated position and punished.

How Scapegoating Works

The purpose of a scapegoat is to pass blame onto someone else. Psychologically abusive parents rid themselves of their troubled character by dumping it onto the scapegoated child, allowing the parents to maintain an image of themselves as healthy. The story the parents tell looks like this: "If it weren't for our one child, our family would be perfectly healthy." Scapegoating enables power-hungry parents to hide behind an appearance of normalcy, ignoring and carefully concealing their pathological and sadistic emotional abuses of their children. If you have been cast as the family scapegoat, the story told of you was especially egregious. All it takes for a negative narrative to start is being a fussy baby. For example, I was told, "You came out screaming and never stopped." When I was a teenager, my mother made it clear she couldn't wait for me to graduate so she wouldn't have to deal with me anymore. What these snide moments of abuse indicated is that at any moment of standing up for myself, having some type of mood or moment my parents didn't want to deal with, or needing support they didn't have the desire to give, the bullying began.

When you are assigned the lowest role in a family, it is excruciating. The disastrous impact it has on your self-image is unimaginable. When you are the scapegoat, you are treated like a thing. A thing that holds little value. You are dehumanized. Dehumanizing is a form of emotional abuse that is seen not only in the microcosm of the family but also in the larger culture. In fact, dehumanizing is active in the larger culture every day, which has led to increased violence, human rights violations, war crimes, and genocide. There are many patterns of parenting that are not currently regarded as abusive. Yet, hidden abuses, such as ostracizing and scapegoating children, are desensitizing and horribly destructive. Being dehumanized forces you to become comfortable being treated as subhuman.

What Distinguishes the Scapegoat from the Rest of the Family?

The child who is scapegoated is chosen because this child bears some threat to the most dominant parent. This child is most often outspoken, sensitive, and empathetic and possesses integrity. They can be agreeable, kind, and conscientious to a fault, which makes them an easy target. They are open and willing to consider other viewpoints, which is extremely threatening to parents who function best without integrity or fairness. The bad child–turned–scapegoat is commonly a truth teller in families where corruption is brewing beneath the perfect family image. The truth in any form is destabilizing to the dysfunction the power-holding parent functions from. This child must be scapegoated and bullied into not exposing the abuse that exists beneath the surface. This lack of truth intensely frustrates the truth-telling child, causing them to act out what they are forbidden to speak out loud and resolve.

Like a cult, emotionally abusive and manipulative parents set absolute rules for their children to never expose the abuses they tolerated from their parents. If you were the scapegoat, it was your duty to keep quiet and remain the scapegoat. As long as you followed the rules, you could earn temporary safety through your obedience and efforts to be "good." However, as soon as you started questioning your parents, it spurred the unwanted threat that you could potentially overthrow their hierarchy in some way. Your emotionally abusive parents most likely used bullying to put you back in what they considered your rightful place.

What an Abusive Parent Gains by Having a Scapegoat

Toxic parents need a scapegoat to avoid taking accountability for what they have done. Instead, they blame the scapegoat. This technique of passing the buck is commonplace with parents who cannot allow their ego to be tainted by an error. They scapegoat and bully for the sport of it. Escaping accountability is incredibly satisfying for tyrannical parents. For them, relationships are no deeper than a game of chess. If they win, even if they must cheat, they are satisfied.

Results of Emotional Abuse on the Scapegoat

Here are the effects of what emotional abuse can do to the scapegoat.

Difficulty Forming Intimate Relationships

It would make sense from being ostracized throughout your childhood that, as an adult, you could struggle with emotional and physical intimacy.

Remedy: Practice being open to love. Being in love doesn't mean dropping your boundaries, but love cannot happen if boundaries make an impenetrable fortress. True vulnerability comes from taking some risks.

Substance Abuse and Other Addictive Behaviors

The stress of being cast as the "bad one" creates a tremendous amount of emotional pain. This pain causes some to turn to drugs or alcohol to numb feelings.

Remedy: Addiction can often be boiled down to a destructive habit of compulsive comfort-seeking. If you are struggling with addiction, seek professional help. Also, explore other ways to find comfort that are life-sustaining, such as meditation, a healthier diet, and exercise.

Social Anxiety

Because children of emotionally abusive parents grew up being dehumanized, many struggle in social settings. You may feel a strong irreverence toward authority and rules, or you may fear authority and what others think of you, for example.

Remedy: I love the saying "Watch your wake." If you're a boat, you do not want your wake to be so enormous that other boats cannot get by, nor do you want your wake to be so small that no one notices you and you get run over. Socially, you want to watch your wake by finding the middle ground between defensiveness and passiveness, both of which are driven by fear.

Unstable Sense of Self

Scapegoats struggle with a severely damaged sense of self because they have been treated like the liability of the family. This low self-esteem often serves as a launchpad for poor decision-making and impulsive behavior.

Remedy: To create inner stability, it is important to take charge of your life. Choose the people you want to have in it and pursue the things you want, dream about, love, and desire. Engaging in the areas of your life that you are most passionate about is empowering. When our self-esteem has some muscle behind it, it calms our senses, makes it easier for us to relate to others, and allows others into our hearts.

If you are a victim of scapegoating, take heart. It is healthy that you couldn't take the abuse anymore and needed to change your circumstances. Let me remind you that you were chosen to be the scapegoat because you have qualities your parents lack. You were chosen because you were threatening. You were chosen because you were powerful. Your parents saw that power in you and wanted to take it away. If you choose to escape or create distance, understand that you will not be allowed to do so freely. You will not receive well wishes or any level of understanding around your decision to create distance, regardless of how obvious the reasons may be. It will be the goal of your egotistical parents to destroy you to get you to fall back under their imprisoning influence.

> **Moment of truth:** The only way for toxic parents to keep the family secrets from being exposed is to ignite a smear campaign against the truth-telling scapegoat.

Get Ready for the Smear Campaign

A family with values based in love, cooperation, and authenticity never produces a scapegoat. Functional parents do not need a scapegoat because they are not ashamed to admit their own weaknesses and seek help when necessary. Emotionally abusive and manipulative parents thrive on having you to blame. They choose to selectively remember the version of you they had the most power over, no matter how long it's been or how much you've changed. Creating distance or cutting off your emotionally abusive parents isn't easy. It's terrifying. As you prepare to face the resulting smear campaign, remember the reasons you doubt or distrust your parents. Remind yourself that you are the only one looking out for you. You are not an idiot nor are you a traitor. You are the child of emotionally abusive parents who deserves freedom, safety, and support.

Moment of truth: Scapegoats exist only in very sick families.

CHAPTER 10

Survive the Smear Campaign

Once you walk out that door, either through having no contact or creating a significant emotional distance between yourself and your parents, get ready for your parents to ignite war. Your emotionally abusive parents fear your transformative powers, as witnessed through your insight to stand up against their bullying. The smear campaign solidifies your role as the forever scapegoat, the deserter. When you are being smeared, your complete annihilation is your parents' goal. You will be publicly humiliated in front of family members and friends. You will be dismissed, shut out, and stonewalled. Your character will be assassinated, and you will be lied about. They will attempt to make you look like a crazy person who has totally become unhinged. Your abusive parents will head this campaign and relentlessly work to drive you over the edge by pushing all your emotional buttons. The smear campaign is your parents' way of igniting damage control. You will be retaliated against for exposing the family secrets.

Their retaliation tactics will be extensive and creative. They will try to exhaust you. Your parents will emotionally blackmail and try to gaslight you into believing that your abuse never occurred. They will accuse you of being unreasonable and overly dramatic. When you stand your ground, they will make the smearing of you even more intense by further silencing you for what makes you so special in the first place—your ability to be discerning, intuitive, and compassionate. Your abusive parent will use your own words and insights as weapons to rewrite history and make you look foolish. They will feast upon your insecurities to ensure you feel too powerless to complain or take further action to expose them. This form of conspiracy may not theoretically be illegal, but it poses great harm to those who are targeted.

The Power of Blind Willfulness (Mob Mentality)

In today's world, we are governed by rules that tell us who and how to be in order to survive in our culture. You are introduced to what rules to follow in your family of origin. The deceitful rules emotionally abusive parents live by create what systems therapists refer to as *myths*. These myths are comparable to the theology or belief systems of many churches and/or governments that argue stridently in support of the validity of their rules and rituals, even when they are clearly absurd. Ignorantly following rules that don't make sense is known as *blind willfulness*, which can be understood as going along to get along. You and all others must be silent to the power-holders (your parents) to avoid conflict because conflict might destroy the system (family).

Triangulation Turns People Against You

Triangulation is the easiest and most effective way for your parents to involve third parties in the smear campaign. The sole intention of triangulation is to turn as many people against you as possible to make you feel socially rejected and alone. Triangulation gives your parents the power to manipulate and govern communication between two parties. This way, the only people with the information that others want to hear are your corrupt parents. Something critical to understand is that your parents and other involved people come together in the smear campaign to protect each other. This type of protection keeps the family in their desired state of imbalance and dysfunction, allowing them to continue pretending nothing is wrong. They come together to convince themselves that they are a strong and united family and that you, the scapegoat, are the problem.

Toxic Parents Cast Themselves as the Victim

In the smear campaign, emotionally abusive parents cast themselves as the victim of you, their child, for one pivotal reason: to twist the story. To avoid exposure, they flip the script. Smear campaigns start off as a delusion. Your parents create a false narrative about the reality of where fault lies in the demise of the relationship between you and them. Your parents choose to deceive themselves about what is real to protect their pride. They convince themselves of all the reasons you deserve their abuse in a manner they can feel good about. In this delusion, your parents present themselves as good, righteous, caring, honest, and innocent people, bemoaning how you are totally out of your mind and cruel, so no one will believe you when you try to expose what they have put you through. Naive, uninformed others fall headfirst into your parents' compelling story, are triangulated without knowing it, and feel tremendous compassion for your "poor" parents. When your parents are spouting off claims that you abused them, are disconnected from reality, aren't like other children, and are totally unstable, the reality your parents are desperately trying to conceal is that they are all the things they accuse you of being.

For example, a young teenager had a tyrannical and controlling mother who would video him while punishing him. His sibling was able to record one of these interactions and shared the video. What was on that video was horrific. This mother was not disciplining. She was enraged, irrational, emotionally abusive, and unfair. She was demeaning, gaslighting, and berating this boy. This boy was made to sit in a chair during this interaction, while she towered over him to further assert her dominance. This mother would record these interactions to make her son feel threatened, afraid, and demoralized. The video would allow her to capture his most defensive moments as evidence to smear him, while conveniently editing out the abuses she enacted upon him that caused his defensive reaction. At one point, during the video, this boy tried to stand up for himself, saying he was the one who should be recording her. She slapped him across the face, demanded he hand over his phone, and promptly placed him on restriction. Clearly, this mother was afraid of having the unedited truth of her being abusive exposed. The story an emotionally abusive parent presents about you to others is a much more accurate depiction of who they are.

To maintain the momentum of the campaign against you, your parents will couch themselves as the victim by presenting only the parts where you reacted to their abuse, as if this is where the story started. To further twist the narrative, they will claim that everything they have ever done has been "in your best interests." They will falsify that out of nowhere, you started being cruel, irrational, and unreasonable. By downplaying their part, they will twist your natural desire to stand up for yourself into a vile act of aggression against them.

> **Moment of truth:** Abusive parents feel deeply threatened when you develop high standards, firm boundaries, and a confident voice.

Why Doesn't Anyone Help the Scapegoat?

Because smear campaigns are led by powerful and scary parents and the fact that people believe parents over children, little mercy is given to the child who is scapegoated. You are left to suffer the storm of emotional terrorism all alone. Even as it becomes clear that the group bullying is taking its toll on you, no one helps you for one primary reason: Others don't want to be associated with you for fear of your parents, their leaders, turning on them. When a group of individuals, such as a family, reaches unanimity without critical reasoning (blind willfulness) or an evaluation of consequences or alternatives for solutions, thinking becomes rigid and fixed.

There is tremendous pressure to fit in one's own family. People, especially children, sacrifice their own ideas, urges, likes, and dislikes to belong. People will die for their families. Culture has evolved to a point where you are freer to self-actualize—that is, to develop wholeness, emotional intelligence, spiritual depth, and self-awareness. However, emotionally abusive parents refuse to keep up with such changes for fear of losing control. This type of blended-group thinking provides family members with the disturbing feeling that if they dare to do anything outside of the control of your parents, doing so will be groundless and wrong. They are too afraid of going beyond what is expected of them and what it would mean for them if they did. It is far easier to go along to get along, which is why the smear campaign is so effective.

However, in the underbelly of the smear campaign, scapegoating is stressful for everyone involved. Scapegoating causes resentment, paralyzing fear, anger, avoidance, guilt, separation, seclusion, and defensiveness for those who follow along with your parents. Why? Because it causes the smear campaign's group members to be part of a dividing and abusive relationship triangle. These types of dynamics are based in polarizing judgments and provoke conflict among family members. There are no winners. Everybody loses. But strategically, just like in any other war, there is strength in numbers. Therefore, those being sucked into the smear campaign choose to align themselves with your parents, instead of helping you survive under the mass shaming and emotionally violent undercurrents.

It is important to recognize that the family members and friends who join the smear campaign are weak. It's easy for any majority to bully and ostracize a single person with the cruel emotional games of one-upmanship and other sadistic behaviors to maintain a psychological advantage that empowers your emotionally sick parents. At the same time, a smear campaign destroys the spiritual growth of the family members and friends who join the gang. This is all for the sole purpose of preserving a false narrative sprouting from your own parents' duplicitous integrity. However, because powerlessness is not something anyone desires to feel, to protect themselves from being scapegoated, these more vulnerable others join in against you, accepting the judgment that you are not well and are inferior to those in the group.

Why Scapegoats Struggle to Save Themselves

The powerful effects of groupthink deeply impact the scapegoat in horrific and debilitating ways. Breaking free from your abusive and manipulative parents forces you to come face-to-face with a fate known as *defamiliarization*. Defamiliarization is terrifying. In the normal course of everyday life, you should feel at home in the world. You should feel safe and connected. Everything in the world that relates to you—objects, people, roles, values, ideals, symbols, organizations, and even the sense of who you are in relationship to the rest of the world—should seem comfortable, familiar, and meaningful. Defamiliarization is an unsettling and destabilizing feeling that all is not well—that the outward appearance of the world (your family) has not been what it was supposed to be.

Once a smear campaign starts, you recognize there is no familiar solid ground underneath you, that perhaps there never was, and this is daunting. As you expose yourself to other possibilities outside of the manipulation and abuse used to keep you connected to and dependent on your parents, you become conflicted between going back to where you feel you are supposed to stay (your family) and exploring other alternatives that seem healthier and happier for you. When the reality of defamiliarization starts settling in, it is paralyzing. Life suddenly feels utterly ludicrous, lacking in meaning and authenticity. You begin to wonder what the point is of pursuing your larger goals in life, which include continuing to stand up against your parents, if it means losing everything and everyone that is familiar (even if toxic) to you.

When you start realizing that all the things that have been preached as gospel by your parents have been far from true, you naturally start turning against yourself. You question whether your desires to be yourself are right or wrong. This doubt pulls you away from the yearnings to live as your most authentic self, causing you to consider going back. You wonder, because you are the only one questioning your abuse, whether maybe there is something off in you and you are wrong to want a different life. You reason that perhaps everyone else is right, and you are misperceiving things; what you are feeling, thinking, witnessing, experiencing, and wanting is not valid but selfish; and maybe you are crazy. It is easy to fall into crushing feelings of guilt when you have decided to do life differently, fearful that wanting this has been too bold of an overstepping of the constraints placed upon you by your parents and the larger culture.

However, the truth is what it is, and it will continue to surface from within you. The truth brings about a raw admission to yourself that there was always some type of invisible barrier between yourself and your parents. I remember specifically telling my mother I was nothing like her or my sibling, and I didn't fit with them. I was different. This feeling of being an outsider leaves you feeling nebulous, empty, and unclear about the scope of your life, identity, perception of your parents and other family members, and outsider role in the family. If all your family members seemingly fit perfectly together, you deduce that something must be wrong with you, or you would fit too.

It is for all these reasons the smear campaign is used. It is used to torture you into submission by capitalizing on your self-doubt to kill your dreams for a different life. The smear campaign has the intention of convincing you that it is much safer to stay in or go back to the old familiar, albeit abusive, family environment, even when you know staying or going back will cause you tremendous harm. Sadly, we are the most attracted to and feel the safest with what we are most familiar with, including people, even when who or what we are familiar with is poisonous and unhealthy.

The Psychological Pull of Familiarity

The emotional influence of the familiarity of your parents has a powerful hold over you, in both your mind and your heart. People in general fear the idea of complete freedom. If you can do whatever pleases you, you fear that you could make some terrible mistakes. If you did make an irreparable mistake and leave all that is familiar to you, who will you turn to if you fail? I felt this way for decades before finding the courage to escape. If I failed, it would prove my parents right. I would also have nowhere to go because separating myself from them was something I did to myself. It would be my fault and my deserved consequences. However, the abuse was so bad that I still made the terrifying choice to choose me. I had to. There was no other viable choice.

> **Moment of truth:** Sometimes it is what feels like the most unsafe choices that bring you to safety.

Because you have chosen to protect your life with boundaries, your parents and other involved family members view this as the ultimate betrayal. They don't want you to have anyone to turn to. They believe you deserve to be all alone and without support. It is truly this sadistic. Your parents hold a deep resentment toward you for seeing through the charade they spent every waking minute perfecting to cover up their poor character. The more energy your parent must expend in lying about you, the more hatred they feel toward you. This unfounded hatred leaves you feeling isolated. When it is your own parents leading the campaign of abuse, nothing seems to stop the darkness of their cruelty from seeping in and damaging your soul.

Your desire to feel love and remorse from your parents is another reason others won't step in to help you. Outsiders see it as your job to rescue yourself by working harder to win the affections of your parent by being "good." This thought process perpetuates your abuse. The pressure placed on you to make peace—to do all the hard work and labor of reconciliation and forgiveness—makes it even harder to save yourself. For example, a teenage boy shared, "If I believed all the horrible things my mom said to me about who I am, I would literally believe I was Satan." He also shared, "Before I decide to move in with my dad, I just want to see how long I can take it [his mother's abuse]." This desire to "take it" comes from wanting things to be different than they are. Hoping for things to be different to avoid feeling the pain of your parents' rejection causes you to cling to parents who abuse you. Unfortunately, this wish keeps you in the denial of the reality of how abusive your parents are, which blocks you from grieving. Instead of saving yourself, you remain stuck wanting and wishing for things to get better. Unfortunately, things don't get better when you are the scapegoat. This is the role you have been assigned.

Steps to Saving Yourself from a Smear Campaign

If you are the victim of an emotionally violent smear campaign, here are some strategies to help you.

- Do not try and defend yourself against the blatant lies being told about you.

- Stay quiet and let the smear campaign run its course.

- Trust the power of your truth. It will come out in its own time and at the exact right time.

- Take the opportunity, while the smear campaign is active, to move on with your life.

- Observe who falls into the mob mentality and who sticks by your side. This is important information.

- Stay grounded, even though it hurts. This too shall pass.

- Trust that the truth is like cream in coffee, it will eventually rise to the surface.

Moment of truth: After too much bad has happened, you will feel compelled to live your truth because you can no longer participate in the lie.

CHAPTER 11

When the Scapegoat Fights Back

All people have a natural yearning for a sense of agency and control over their own life. As the family scapegoat, you have been robbed of this right. However, in a beautiful twist of irony, the yearning for freedom is felt more powerfully in the scapegoat. Your toxic parents pushed your limits with a reckless entitlement. They did not view you as deserving of any rights. As far as they're concerned, they own you simply because they are your parents. They failed to realize, however, that one day you would become powerful enough to disown them. The desire for your freedom will eventually override your fear.

Escape Being the Scapegoat

You can't avoid how you are labeled, how your parents treat you, what dishonesties they spread, or who they involve to further denigrate you. Escaping the role of the scapegoat comes down to how much you allow yourself to react and engage in the drama your parents create. The more concerned you are about the smear campaign, what is being said, and who is involved, the more disempowered you become in creating the emotional distance you need to change your life. Physical distance can help, with many scapegoats choosing to move a great distance away from their parents, but being emotionally invested is where your true vulnerability is.

Try not to be too hard on yourself about the things your parents say and do. Whether you stay around them or set boundaries to create space, either decision will be used against you. You are damned if you do and damned if you don't, so you may as well do what is best for you. No matter what you do, your parents will continue to see you as the root cause of their problems. You will not escape being the scapegoat in their mind. You must escape the role in your own mind. It is not about controlling them anymore. It is about taking control of your reactions to them. You did not set healthy boundaries to stay stuck in a dysfunctional life.

Responding to Intentionally Provoked Emotional Reactions

When your emotionally abusive parents intentionally attempt to provoke an emotional reaction from you, you can choose how to respond. Here are some ways you can support yourself and bolster your ability to respond in the way that you'd like to.

Proactively Set Boundaries

Somewhere inside of your parents, your being passive to their abuse shows a willingness to take it, which enrages them even more. Protect yourself with firm, definitive boundaries.

Remain Quiet

Do not fight force with force. Instead of standing against your parents, stand for yourself. Your truth is best observed through your silence.

Give Yourself Healing Reminders

You are not the terrible, mentally unwell person your parents have made you out to be. You are capable, are worthy, and have everything it takes to live your own life. Remind yourself that you get nowhere in life screaming.

Take Your Power Back

Each time your parents assassinate your character, do not give them the pleasure of seeing your broken emotional carcass lying in front them. Instead, make sure they see your resurrected self. Everywhere they look, like a recurring dream, live in a way where they see you thriving.

Remember That Revenge Is Wasteful

It is okay to pass through wanting revenge, but it is even more powerful not to seek it.

I was recently given an opportunity for revenge from someone in my family who became the scapegoat after I left. The information this person sent me was deeply incriminating and detailed the most disgusting evil levels of betrayal put into motion by those in my family. This person, without my interest or consent, sent me evidence in writing, photos, emails, and texts of how my parent and another family member had lied to and betrayed this person. The kind of destruction I could have enacted with this information was monumental. This is exactly why this person reached for me, to get me—the child who escaped and writes the books, the first scapegoat—on their team as a power play against their abusers.

However, the level of this person's own selfishness was also extremely clear. This person was trying to seduce me with my own pain to jump back into the abuse, chaos, and drama I fought my entire life to escape to meet their own needs. This person had stood complicit to my abuse for as long as this person was in my life. This person was a willing contributor to my scapegoated position who had tossed me in the middle of their problems with my family members, just as they were attempting to do in this new situation. However, I now have zero room in my heart for revenge plots and emotional power plays. To protect my own heart, I blocked this person from contacting me any further and was ready to send a cease-and-desist letter if this person continued to pursue my support.

This person's pain and my family's involvement in it is not my story to tell, nor is it my problem to fix. I highly encourage you to refrain from seeking revenge when dealing with parents and other involved family members who have harmed you. Trust that true justice can be better served by higher forces. The blessing of this deeply triggering experience is knowing that absolutely nothing about those in my family has changed, my most toxic parent is still at the helm, and, in fact, it seems they have all only grown to become even more corrupt.

Hold Your Solid Ground

The bitterness your parent feels toward you is strong, and I am certain it has deeply scarred you. However, it is up to you to no longer allow anyone to throw their emotional garbage into your yard. You are not your parents' emotional janitor. They can pick up their own messes.

Be Gentle with Yourself

When your parents are cruel to you, it is common to learn to be equally as cruel and cutting to yourself. It is hard to create an abundant life from this place.

Remind yourself that many interesting people in the world lived hard lives. You are not alone, and the pain caused to you is not your fault. Find fellow scapegoats and connect with them. The validation you have always craved will be there. They will help you see your own suffering as reflected in their own experiences. A special someone wrote me the following note.

"Hi Dr. Sherrie, I have no idea if this message will make it to you, but I'm 41 and about a week ago was contemplating not wanting to stay on this Earth. Not sleeping and anxiety worse than I thought possible. I have had your book in my Amazon cart for well over six months. I finally ordered it, have spent this week reading it, and I am almost finished with it. I called a therapist, which I probably should have done a long time ago. Really what I wanted to say is I'm sorry and thank you. Sorry for what I know you've gone through because I know your pain. I don't wish it upon anyone and reading your book I was like, yup

I'm definitely not alone! The thank you is for the books, your social media platforms, and sharing your story...sometimes, well pretty much daily right now, your words become my affirmations and are the reasons I get through the day."

Finding this type of moral and emotional support is integral to your healing because it provides you with a sense of what you have always yearned for: a sense of belonging. Loneliness and sorrow walk hand in hand when you're the scapegoat. If you switch your perspective, though, you will see that others around you are holding the same lonely hand that you are. And, just like that, you have each other to hold on to.

Protect Your Well-Being

There are many scapegoats who stay stuck in their traumatic story and don't heal. Do not allow this to be you. Your new motto for healing: "Feel. Deal. Heal." Feel what you need to feel. Deal with the reality of your circumstances by accepting them for what they are. Heal by implementing strategies that move you more deeply into the soothing of your soul. No reaction from you, no reward for your parents.

Know Who You Are

Toxic parents teach you that you are someone you are not. You believe them because they are your parents. The path to loving yourself comes through getting to know who you are. Your personal narrative—the unique story of your life—is something you should have been allowed to author yourself from your very beginning. To explore who you are, I highly recommend journaling. In a journal, you can write on your own. You can be yourself for once. You can enjoy and respect the privacy of it. No one is watching. No one is criticizing. No one is judging. Nobody is weighing in on you. It's just you in conversation with yourself. With a journal, you can write—and right—yourself back into existence.

Take a Breath

When you are in fear, you reflexively take short, shallow breaths, which limits your ability to think clearly. When feeling fearful or anxious, learn to take a minute. When you pause, give yourself time to breathe. Pausing offers you clarity on where and how to start, big or small, to grow yourself to the next level.

Self-Examine

If you are not aware of which vulnerabilities of yours are the easiest to exploit, you cannot know how to protect yourself. Discover which feelings and behaviors make you potential prey by noticing when you're emanating a spirit of weakness rather than strength out into the world. It is imperative to govern your mind and heart to stay committed to thinking and reacting rationally. Unlike your abusive and manipulative parents and other involved family and friends, commit to the awareness that until you are right within, you cannot get anywhere outwardly. You did not ever deserve to be extinguished by your parents. No one deserves that. All of nature's children have a right to exist, be loved, and grow, each in their own unique way.

See the Good in Yourself

This quote from the movie *Pretty Woman* says it all: "People put you down enough you start to believe it… The bad stuff is easier to believe. You ever notice that?" Take moments to feel proud of yourself. Treat your life as sacred. When you do this, you will hold no regret over the parents and other involved family members and friends you had to distance yourself from or remove from your life. Stay true to yourself. You are the sole person who decides the fate of your life. If no one is lending you a helping hand, oh well. You've got this.

When you start the process of saving your own life, keep in mind the ground your parents and other involved family and friends stand on isn't solid. The ground they stand on has no value because it is built upon lies, which hold no power in the long term. Lies have only short-term power. The smear campaign is fragile. It can function only on quantity, not quality. A lie is so low quality that it will always need more. It will demand your parents' constant work, grooming, additions, embellishments, and conversations to keep it in motion. The truth is totally different. It stops traffic without making a noise. When you see the lie burning through your life like a forest fire taking everything in its path, remember it is taking everything down, except for the person who holds the truth, which is you. The truth of your abuse cannot be extinguished, no matter how hard your parents may try.

From Scapegoat to Escape GOAT

When you fight back as the scapegoat, you position yourself to become your own superhero. If you think about it, all superheroes have valiant enemies. A superhero would never know how strong they are if there weren't an adversary to compare themselves to. In superhero stories, it is good versus evil. Nearly all superheroes fail to succeed at first. In every superhero story, you are left sitting on the edge of your seat, consumed with worry, fearing the superhero will not pull through and get an edge over those seeking to destroy them. This means there is a learning curve for all superheroes. Your parents and others who invest in scapegoating you lack morals and basic human decency. They operate on malice. This is not you. These are not the weapons you use. You don't need weapons. You are the weapon. The weapon of truth.

Like with every superhero, your greatest adversaries will be those who are the closest to you, the ones you would least expect. This is why they are your greatest adversaries. They will betray you the deepest and test your truth to the core, only to reveal the validity of your truth time and again. It will be your enemies who most powerfully and clearly expose the goodness of your character. Ironically, it will also be your enemies who most clearly expose their own cruelty and malice. Your parents, who choose to be your enemy, will watch you come out on top, no matter how disparaging they may have perceived themselves to be toward you. You are destined for bigger things. The hope for your deserved destiny has always been calling to you, or you would have never fled the control of your parents and their posse.

You are not the sacrificial lamb. Your role in this world will never again include "emotional trash can." You are not the instigator you have long been accused of being. You are not the person who has caused the problems in the family. Rather, you are fighting for your belief in justice. There is no point in continuing to tolerate parents who lack basic human civility and did not defend you when you needed it. Instead, you choose to fight for yourself. Some of the most precious things you value are an adherence to reality, authenticity, and integrity. This adherence to justice makes you a GOAT (greatest of all time).

Those who live from the essence of what is true, sincere, and genuine are considered GOATs. You were once cast as the "bad one," but choosing freedom, in whatever form that is fitting for you, allows you to discover that you were a GOAT all along. You understand, without a shadow of doubt, that you were raised by emotionally abusive parents who were so full of hate that they had to gain feelings of power by terrifying you and abandoning you in dark, horrible places. It is this insight that makes you invincible. It is your natural commitment to truth, justice, and fairness that was held captive and suppressed under an authoritarian parental regime, where your only role in that system was that of the loser. You are no loser. You are the greatest of all time in the most humble, remarkable, and magical ways because you are a truth teller, one of earth's angels. Angels aren't meant to live in hell. You have the power to create heaven from the ashes of your old life. If you spend enough time in pain, it will eventually introduce you to your joy. Rest assured, karma does come for those who conspire against you—and predators like your parents are eventually exposed. No matter what roles you may have been forced to play in your family, they will not matter when you make moves, such as setting boundaries, that propel you into your own greatness.

Moment of truth: Horrific abuse and manipulation ran in your family, until it ran into you. You have been chosen to break the cycle.

CHAPTER 12

Start Choosing You

The first years of distance between yourself and your parents place you in what I refer to as no-man's-land. If you have reached no-man's-land, congratulations! If you're not there yet or are new to this place, treat yourself with grace. Trust that you are on the right journey for you. Making it here means you have fought hard to put the proper limits in place to protect yourself. This is your first and most significant win on the path toward healing, even if you feel beaten and battered beyond comprehension. You. Are. Still. Here. You have fought valiantly.

In no-man's-land, you are acutely aware that the smearing of you has not and will not stop simply because you made it across the border. In fact, the violence of the campaign will be at its ugliest. You are the most vulnerable to going back to your old life in these first few years in no-man's-land. It's okay. All superheroes get tested at each new step in their journey. It is totally normal to feel pulled back by the depth, voracity, length, and complete insanity of the smear campaign. The sadistic nature of the smear campaign has likely been enough to deplete you, to isolate and destroy any hope you have in life and people, making you fear the unknown life ahead of you that you are fighting so hard for. It is normal to question whether any of what you have done to save yourself has been or will ever be worth the pain, aloneness, and rejection you continue to face. As a survivor, I can share that all of us come out of the extremes of parental abuse, alienation, and smear campaigning a different person. You will never be the same person you were before. This is a good thing.

In no-man's-land, you are stuck between the life you had with your emotionally abusive parents and those who were complicit and the unfamiliarity of the life in front of you. Life feels quite empty in no-man's-land, aside from all the chaos, emotion, and unfamiliar change to navigate. Good news: There is much value in this space between lives if you can hold on to yourself. You have plenty of time now. You're out. All superheroes need to rest, and that is what no-man's-land is for. No-man's-land gives you time to think, feel, assimilate, adjust, restore, and breathe. You are well aware the smear campaign will haunt you from the shadows for the remainder of your life. In getting here, though, you have developed certain skill sets you can count on to largely mute the war waged against you. The work you need to do now is internal. As afraid as you may start off in no-man's-land, remind yourself that you have already walked through and witnessed the true depths of hell and have survived the vilest and most disgusting of human behaviors.

No-man's-land offers up some of the most important gems to elevate your healing and prepare you for your future. The most critical transformation to make in no-man's-land is the psychological movement from the disempowered victim to the empowered survivor.

No-man's-land isn't a place you want to stay stuck. If you get stuck here, you remain a victim of your past, never embracing the amazing life you have the opportunity and power to create. If you stay stuck, you will remain living a small, negative, bitter, afraid, lonely, and angry existence. You will hate people and believe you can trust no one. This is the exact goal your parents had for you in daring to distance yourself from them. If you stay stuck, the only difference between your old life and this one is that in this one you now take over as the warden of your own emotional prison. Staying stuck is a choice. Staying stuck keeps you behind the bars of powerlessness, where you replay the sad story of your life over and over in your mind and retell it in great detail to any available listener. You choose to retraumatize yourself with each retelling. This type of powerlessness will find a way to seep into every area of your life. The choice to stay stuck will not lead you to a better life. To get unstuck, you must work through the complexities of relentless hope.

Relentless Hope

In no-man's-land, one of your biggest objectives is to let go of any hope you may still carry for your toxic parents to wake up, right their wrongs, and validate your abuse as real. Some stay in no-man's-land relentlessly hoping for this awakening in their parents to occur. Living in relentless hope is confusing and re-wounding at best because you are placing hope in the hopeless. You come by this relentless hope honestly because you have been parented to feel this type of hope since your earliest memories. However, your manipulative parents intentionally frustrated the purity of your hope in them.

Hope is not an emotion your parents should have ever manipulated for sport. Hope that reaches its limit turns to hate. Toxic parents deserve the hate they provoked in you because it was your hate they were seeking. When parents are sick enough to toy with hope, they destroy it. Hate steps in to protect hope. Hate enters to take control and gain momentum against the abuses being doled out, to bring an end or closure to them. Hate cut through your confusion and helped you stand up for yourself. You started to hate your parents because you wanted them to acknowledge your pain. You hated because your hurt mattered, and you wanted that known. You wanted your parents to wake up.

Being ruthlessly provoked by your parents to show your hate filled them with a sick sense of accomplishment. The intent behind the smear campaign was, and is, to accomplish just this. They want to continue to provoke your hateful reactions to cement you as the bad guy long after you have created the distance you need from them. You are branded the selfish child who hates their parents. From the reflective vantage point of no-man's-land, you can look back and see that the battles won by your parents were nearly always followed up with their showing kindness toward you once again. They moved on from your hate and pain as if nothing had happened. Those breadcrumbs of conditional kindness brought relief and placed you in the hard swing back to a state of relentless hope again, even more deeply. That back-and-forth swinging from hope to hate continued throughout your life until enough was enough.

Something that became clear in my time in no-man's-land is that it is nearly impossible for a child or even an adult child to genuinely hate their parent because as their child, you want more than anything to love them and for them to love you back. I recognized that I have hurt far more over my sadistic parents than I have ever hated them. Hate is designed to be acute, or short-lived, because it is not in alignment with who you are in your spirit. What your parents failed to recognize is that hate could and would serve you when used correctly. Hate is filled with movement. Hate propelled you to move your feet away from their abuse. However, because hate is such a grotesque waste of energy long term, in no-man's-land, you will feel compelled to rid yourself of it as quickly as possible—especially once you accept there is no hope to continue to hold in your emotionally abusive parents.

Moment of truth: When you free yourself of the source (parents), you free yourself of the reaction (hate).

Here are some ways to release relentless hope.

- Be honest with yourself about the reality of who your parents are and the abusive ways in which they have treated you.

- Stay true to boundaries you set and distance you create.

- Give yourself something new to hope for by planning and envisioning your life without having to navigate the pressures of emotional games, guilt, neglect, and gossip—all of which exhaust your time, love, focus, and energy.

- Get back out there by making one small new decision toward your freedom after another. Baby steps are steps.

Undoing Years of Brainwashing

Before the clarity of your new life can begin, no-man's-land allows you time to heal from the false things you have been brainwashed to believe about yourself, life, and people. Brainwashing is the process by which your parents pressured you into adopting a radically negative and fearful belief about them, yourself, your safety, and your survival in a systematic and forcible manner. You were programmed to believe that their overreaching critical and negativistic opinions of you were real.

Now that you have the necessary distance to heal, consider that who you are can be found only in how you feel, not in another's opinion of you. Emotions and thoughts, including opinions, are fundamentally different. Toxic parents function best in the mental arena of their opinion of what is right or wrong. They do not care how you feel. They know the truth of who you are resides in the depth of your emotions, which is why they methodically dismiss what you feel. No-man's-land gives you the time and space to reflect on the idea that thoughts and opinions are learned (brainwashing), whereas emotions simply are what they are (truth). Therefore, your parents have never had the right to say what you feel is right or wrong.

When parents do not care about how you feel, there can be no connection. There is no language of "love" between two people without both caring how the other feels. There can be no growth, insight, or meaningful change. When there is no love language between yourself and your parents, there can be no valuable existence for you to hold in their life, or for them to hold in yours. There is nothing universally human connecting you to them or them to you without love. Did you ever notice as you were growing up that your feelings did not go away just because your parents didn't like them? In fact, the more your feelings were dismissed, the more deeply they grew.

Here is the miracle: The truth that drove your feelings to the surface eventually grew strong enough to overpower the negative influence of your parents. When you allow your feelings, you allow your truth. Emotions are the only things powerful enough to change thoughts. When you take time to get out of your head and into your heart, the brainwashing you have undergone is easier to unravel. As you recover and gather your wits in no-man's-land, it becomes clear that the truth of what you felt inside was always fighting for you. It was the correctness of your feelings that gave you the power to stand against your abuse. Somehow, some way, you arrived at the place where you would rather be alone, ostracized, without support, and ganged up on rather than stay under their rule.

This is powerful.

Emotions Are Healthy Until You Are Forced to Repress Them

As you heal in no-man's-land, it is important to understand emotions for what they are in reality before moving into the next phase of your life. Understanding your emotions is to understand yourself. You pass through the energy of emotions—they are not designed to be chronic states of being. Here are some examples of what can happen when you repress certain emotions.

- Sadness is healthy. However, repressed sadness turns into depression. Depression is not healthy.

- Anger is healthy. However, repressed anger turns into rage. Rage is not healthy.

- Love is healthy. However, repressed love turns into possession. Possession, the desire to own and control another human being, is not healthy. Possession is how emotionally abusive parents "love."

- Envy is healthy. However, repressed envy turns into jealousy. Jealousy is not healthy. In fact, jealousy may be the most violent of all the emotions. There are far too many parents who feel jealous of their children. In general, sick people seek to destroy the people they are jealous of.

- Fear is healthy. However, repressed fear turns into anxiety. Chronic anxiety is not healthy.

- Acceptance is healthy. However, repressed acceptance turns into bitterness. Bitterness is not healthy. Bitterness halts forward-moving progress.

It is nearly impossible to understand or get to know your naturally occurring emotions when they have consistently been rejected. When your parents rejected your most authentic feelings, they rejected who you are. Parental abuse and rejection disconnect you from your inner world, causing you to live as a shell of the person you were born to be. Imagine how much lighter your life would feel if you experienced freedom from feelings such as depression, rage, possession, jealousy, anxiety, and bitterness. Many of you may have numbed yourself to chronically negative emotional states, but numbing yourself could possibly morph you into being a negative, hopeless person overall. This is not who you are destined to be, unless you choose so. There is no way to fully disconnect from the sadness of your lived experience throughout childhood. It is a forever and necessary part of you. You can, however, choose what kind of story you tell from this moment forward.

Emotions in their healthy states are energy in motion ("e-motion"). They tell the story of the You you know is inside you. The powerful energy holds the You inside of you who has always known and whispered the truth to you. It is the You inside of you who risked everything to expose your abuse and live your truth. It is the You inside of you who is awake and still fighting for your basic human rights. Have you ever noticed the one emotion your parents punished the most was your anger? Do you know why? Because healthy anger speaks the truth and is powerful enough to bring justice to an injustice.

The Curative and Protective Gifts of Healthy Anger

Anger is a critically important emotion because anger is the first emotion to signal you when someone has crossed a line they should not have. Anger's job is to protect you against a perceived threat, providing a boost of energy (inner power) that gives you the extra strength you need to make you feel a little bigger, bolder, and more confident. Anger creates an imposing armor between you and the rest of the world, allowing you to stand firm on your values when called to do so. Anger clears the way for courage, helping you voice the most difficult truths you previously had been unable to express. Anger gives you the power to say what you need to say and mean it. Anger is an important part of the process of setting yourself free and moving into your new life from no-man's-land. When boundaries are firm and you trust yourself to keep them, the anger you feel naturally fades away.

Moment of truth: Your anger is a part of the You who loves you.

Anger doesn't make you mean or bad. It makes you human. As Maya Angelou told Dave Chappelle (2006):

"You should be angry. You must not be bitter. Bitterness is like cancer. It eats upon the host. It doesn't do anything to the object of its displeasure. So, use that anger. You write it. You paint it. You dance it. You march it. You vote it. You do everything about it. You talk it. Never stop talking it."

Moving from Anger to Resolve

Taking the proper time to care for yourself in no-man's-land allows your anger to transmute from its bold energy and fast-paced momentum into deep feelings of calm, clear resolve. In the last interaction I had with my mother over a meaningless mistake she and the current man in her life made, she coercively turned the moment into a dramatic and irreparable abuse of me. In that moment, I reached the end of what I was ever willing to tolerate from her again. It was clear that if something so meaningless (her following the wrong car to a restaurant) could turn into something so catastrophic and annihilating of my character, I knew that if I continued in a relationship with her, this would be how the rest of my life would continue to play out. This awakening moved me from the maddening and powerless frustration that drove my anger and strong dislike for her to a place of profound resolve. This situation was all the evidence I needed to know that things would never get better between us, because she would never be better. Looking back from no-man's-land, I could see so clearly that my mother has always had the agenda to destroy and humiliate me any chance she could throughout my entire life. Making me hate her was the drug that satisfied her most. She systematically provoked the expression of my ugliest hurts and most damaged feelings. She saw the power she had to make me hate her, and she relished it. It allowed her to put the spotlight of shame on me. She did this to disempower me. It worked for nearly five decades.

What I know now is that the emotion of hate isn't designed to be chronic. However, chronic abuse leaves you with little other choice to feel any differently. The feeling of hurtful hate didn't allow me to grow as a person. It poisoned me. It darkened my heart and dulled my truth. I understand that the hate my mother made me feel for her was a manifestation of her hate for me. I have always felt her disgust for me lurking beneath the surface of her feigned love. The resolve that came from that last abusive moment made the hate in my heart lift. That last moment killed all remaining remnants of any hope I still had, leading me directly into the clarity of my truth. Resolve took over for the hate and pulled me out of my head (her brainwashing) and placed me back in my heart (my truth).

The feeling of resolve answered my questions and cleared my confusion. It was pure. I knew, in the deepest part of my being, that this would be the last time I would ever be at the mercy of my mother and her emotional games. I had had this same type of moment, although not quite as intensely, with my father and sibling five years earlier. There is not a more painful relationship for a child to lose than the one with a parent. However, the divinity of the resolve that graced me in each of the final moments with my parents and sibling came from their disdain for me. The ugliness of abuse did not come from me. It was my audacity to tell the truth that gave them the full stage to show me just how deeply ugly each of them could be. In a strange way, it was the clarity of my own abuse in those last moments with each of them that propelled me into a state of radical acceptance of who they all are, allowing me to let go of my attachments to them. They are emotionally abusive and manipulative people. I remain eternally grateful that the grotesqueness of their behavior made it so clear that it would be okay for me to set boundaries and let go.

In no-man's-land, it is this resolve that made me aware I was exactly where I needed to be. I would rather be parentless and sibling-less than manipulated, used, and abused. I can cope far greater with the hurt and pain of not having them in my life than I was ever able to sustain with them in my life. Resolve opened the door to my new life and closed the door on the old. The resolve I felt was peaceful and offered a soothing tenderness to my closed and wounded heart. It granted me the permission to free myself from decades of pent-up self-protection, maladaptive guilt, anger, hatred, overfunctioning, confusion, and pure sorrow.

Embracing Rebellious Hope

Toxic parents are like a cancer. Cancer is a disease caused when poisonous cells divide uncontrollably and spread into the surrounding healthy tissues, infecting them, too often with no cure. Emotionally abusive parents are no different. They spread their poison throughout your psyche while raising you and continue to spread their emotional cancer through the voraciousness of the smear campaign, creating emotional "dis-ease" (a lack of ease or safety) in your life. There is no treatment or cure for parents who take full advantage of and abuse the vulnerability of their children. This leaves you to be your own cure.

The first step to curing yourself is to decrease your exposure to the emotional cancer. This is where rebellious hope comes in. *Rebellious hope* is a term coined by Dame Deborah James to highlight her determination to beat her cancer and not allow it to control her life. The same follows for you with the emotional cancer of your parents. One of the most beautiful things to reconnect with in no-man's-land is the magical energy of rebellious hope.

Rebellious hope is to have hope in yourself. Hope in the strength and tenacity of your spirit. Rebellious hope is strong enough to stop the abusive and intimidating control your parents want over your life. Rebellious hope is the driving force that keeps you moving forward. It is the energy that holds you close when you lose sight, clearing your path toward love. It is about surrendering, accepting, and allowing truth to be your solution. This kind of hope has a cascading effect: Rebellious hope brings resolve, resolve brings clarity, clarity brings boundaries, and boundaries return you to peace. With boundaries in place, peace can thrive. When peace thrives, rebellious hope continues to regenerate.

With *relentless* hope, which we talked about earlier, you live from fear. You still believe that there is something you can do to make your parents happy. You have tried to love them, but they have never tried to love you. When the innocence of hope is relentless, you never give up. You try harder.

Rebellious hope, on the other hand, tells you when enough is enough. When you embrace rebellious hope, you're more than willing to be cast out if it will set you free of your chronic pain. When this happens, you can detach yourself from relentless hope and be inspired to take a new and healthier direction. This also can help you accept the abusive relationship with your parents for what it is: something that aggravates and provokes your pain.

In no-man's-land, you must look inside and cease the dreaming of what could have or should have been for you with your parents. Instead of giving you the dream they owed you, they chose to deliver you a nightmare. The dream of love and security, although reasonably expected, is not to be found in your parents, but inside of you. Look outside of your parents, gaze into your own face, and give yourself the dream you never received. Honor the love and protection of your rebellious hope. It has been the rebellious hope inside of you that has sustained you all along. This rebellious hope has been there in your lowest moments. It has helped you get back up and finally create the distance you have needed for so long. If you're going to have hope, have rebellious hope in yourself.

CHAPTER 13

Recovering a Source of Power

No-man's-land gives you the space to be reintroduced to yourself. It is such a beautiful thing to see yourself without the lens of darkness blocking you from the purity of who you really are. No-man's-land is a place of recovery and discovery. What your parents manipulated away from you was you being You, just as you are. Your authentic self is made up of the essential qualities of your person, the things that distinguish you as uniquely different from others. Your authentic self is expressed through, but is also solid beyond, factors that include your occupation, relationships, race, age, gender, income, and most importantly your parents. At its core, your authentic self is resilient to the influence of others, including your parents, or you never would have landed in no-man's-land. Your authentic self is your rebellious hope. It is the superhero who has always been advocating for your revival. Your authentic self is the person you have always been in the privacy of your secret garden. It is and has always been calling to you and beckoning you inward. It's the whispers from deep inside telling you what your truth is. In no-man's-land, these whispers become your voice.

Childhood is when you should have been able to have been your most authentic self. All children naturally act and react from emotion. Children are genuinely unabashed and free-spirited. Sadly, your parents did all they could to squash your free-spirited nature. They placed you under their control, making sure you knew how repulsed and embarrassed they felt when you were not consistently being harnessed in, behaving perfectly, being easier, and making them look like good parents. Through their control, you were forced away from being yourself. From childhood, and for many of you long into adulthood, you learned what was expected of you (even when you didn't want to do it), what the right responses were (even when it was not your truth), what was acceptable (even when it was not acceptable to you), and what was desired (even when it didn't bring you joy). As this process continued, you became more disconnected from your authentic self, in exchange for any mustard seed of attachment to the people who raised you.

> **Moment of truth:** Children are born knowing love. When a parent mistreats a child, the child doesn't stop loving their parents. The child stops loving themselves.

Trauma research has shown time and again that when people are given the choice between attachment and authenticity, people naturally choose attachment. Authenticity, from this vantage point, is confused with performing for or earning love. Too many of you believe if you do not work hard for love, you will be abandoned. You stopped loving yourself because your parents taught you that you are not worthy of love. You reason that had you been easier to love, your parents would have loved you. Believing you are not lovable sets you up to develop and live with an unconscious but powerful resistance to happiness. How can you feel something (happiness) you don't believe you deserve to feel or have?

Understanding a Resistance to Happiness

When raised in a negativistic, unsafe environment, where happiness was not a part of daily life, happiness ceases to exist. In no-man's-land, it will become crystal clear how the negativistic environment you were raised in was cancerous to your human spirit. You start to see how when your parent punished you, you learned to punish yourself. When your parent nitpicked you, you learned to nitpick yourself. When your parent emotionally neglected or abandoned you, you learned to emotionally neglect and abandon yourself. When your parents showed you hate and disgust, you learned to hate and be disgusted with yourself. When your parents showed you very little love, you believed you were not lovable. When your parent failed to follow through, you learned to view yourself as unimportant. When your parent talked poorly about you, you learned to talk poorly to and about yourself. When your parent didn't believe in you, you learned not to believe in yourself. When your parent betrayed you, you learned to betray yourself. When your parent turned against you, you learned to turn against yourself. The list goes on and on. Children believe their emotionally abusive parents because they are not provided with any refuting evidence.

Under this type of parenting, you were taught that you did not deserve freedom or happiness. Emotionally abusive parents made pain your purpose, instead of happiness. Under their damaging judgment, your default emotion became fear. You have learned to believe that if you want anything good, you have to suffer to obtain it. Toxic parents set you up to fear the negative outcome in all situations. When something good happened, you feared it. You spiraled. You learned to fear that the good things that came your way were just flukes, that you would lose them before even being able to enjoy them. You learned that you shouldn't have had these good things because if you took them, something bad was sure to happen and you would lose them. You habitually leaned into fear because you could not trust that good things, like miracles, could come to you with any ease, with a sense of peace, or with any sense of assuredness or stability.

As the saying goes: Energy flows where your attention goes. Today, it makes sense that you would lean into fear because fear is all you know. When your automatic response is fear, you live from wanting but not having. You unconsciously, but persistently, shoot down the possibility of love and all the wonderful things that manifest from love, such as trust, freedom, unapologetic happiness, miracles, and joy. You live in that defensive hypervigilance trauma (covered earlier) that causes you to misread your environment and project fear and danger into innocent situations.

You try to control things because you're trying to establish feelings of safety and predictability (things you never had growing up) and decrease worry. Yet, the more you feel in control, the more your worries, fears, and frustrations increase and, ironically, the less control you have. This is not a winning formula. No-man's-land gives you the opportunity, time, and space to create a new life formula.

Pain Is Not Your Purpose

What you can embrace in no-man's-land is the idea that pain is not your purpose! The reason pain became your purpose is because your parents taught you a worldview that supports drama, terror, separation, and hardship. You worked hard in the hope of earning love. You were taught that only through suffering could you earn love—but this love didn't exist. For so many of you, suffering had no end date because there was no love to earn, only the illusion of it. It never should have been your responsibility to absorb the pain, disorders, moodiness, and problems of your parents, but as a child you had little other choice. In no-man's-land, the new narrative you are learning to accept and embrace is that pain is not your purpose. Suffering is not a road to living a beautiful, free, and fulfilling life.

The goal in no-man's-land is to start assigning meaning to your suffering—meaning that aligns with the truth of who you really are. You are here to develop new patterns and mindsets that will help you manifest feelings of love, freedom, and stability. When feelings of stability are present, so is safety. Creating this inner shift requires not only a certain amount of faith, but also the willingness and commitment to practice being the person you know that you are and can be. This is the person inside you who your parents did not fully destroy, the part of you that still has hope and a dream of a better, more love-filled life. To be able to practice being who you want to be is a gift. It is the gift of having all the changes you want to make in yourself under your direct control.

Practice Being Who You Want to Be

In no-man's-land, you learn that living authentically requires you stay true to what you feel without judgment. When you allow yourself to feel, you give voice to your experience. You make the story of your pain tangible and real. It means living with an honest expression of your thoughts, feelings, words, and actions. Living authentically also requires the readiness to sacrifice any relationship, situation, or circumstance that diverges from the loving and considerate ways you desire to be treated.

Living authentically takes practice and a lifetime of dedication, fun, creativity, inspiration, and focus. One reason it is not easy to define your authentic self is because this part of you is never static. As a person, you are always evolving, changing, and growing. Being true to the essence of who you are requires consistent attention as you manage the various parts of your personality that make up the wholeness of who you are. Each of these parts is a work in progress in the matrix of your psychosocial development (you will learn the formula for "whole-istic" healing up ahead). For example, the person you are at work is different from the person you are as a parent, friend, family member, or partner. Who you are with strangers may also be different. Each one of these shares a core, but all have different traits and values.

Being authentic is a self-actualizing process. It is not about the kind of self-centeredness you were raised with, where people spewed their negative and judgmental opinions onto you without compassionate or mindful filters. When you're authentic, you are self-aware and equipped with the idea that your opinions are specific to you and your life experience. Not everyone will feel or believe the same as you. You accept this is normal and healthy. Being authentic is to possess the self-awareness to remain humble, open, and discerning when collaborating with others. It is a worthy and precious endeavor to strive to know yourself beyond the meaningless version of who you are that your parents assigned to you.

Practice Enlivening Your Character

Living as your authentic self means being yourself, regardless of whether your parents or others approve. So, you must ask, who is that person inside of you who still dreams of a better life and could use a little magic? What does this inner person, who has been inside you hiding, look like?

The following three-step self-actualizing process is designed to help you discover and explore this inner person.

Make a List of Traits You Want to Strive For

The first step is to make a list of the things you imagine a mature adult looks like, the kind of person and parent you could admire and strive to become. Your list may include traits such as fair, open, emotionally available, disciplined, responsible, humble, composed, discerning, confident, happy, loving, carefree, capable, reasonable, and strong.

Look Up the Definition of Each Word

The second step is to study the words on your list and their definitions. See how they feel inside and envision them being a consistent part of every area of your life, including your words and actions.

Live Each Word

The third step is to start living each word. Practice one word at time, consciously practicing becoming the embodiment of the definition of each word physically, emotionally, mentally, spiritually, relationally, and financially. This practice of assimilating words and definitions into the fabric of who you are as a person is one of the most self-actualizing practices you can take part in. I encourage you to view each word that you assimilate into your being as a rebirth into the high-value human being you were born to be. For example, the word "composure" means a state of being and feeling calm and in control of yourself. If you select this word, allow it to live through your personality in every area of your life, including your actions. For example, eat, speak, communicate, dress, and walk with composure.

Practice Living These Traits

Following this simple, three-step practice can help you become the miracle you were born to be and embody the person you feel is true to you. When you commit to living these traits, they become a natural part of who you are and how you act. The power to move on and heal your life exists inside of you, or you wouldn't be here, recovering and rediscovering your life. With boundaries set, you have the space and time to reacquaint yourself with that quiet force within you that knows when to act, when to move, and when to remain quiet. The part of you that gives you the discernment to lead you to safety. That voice inside that gives you the strength and clarity to do what needs to be done, even when it is excruciating. That inner power that keeps you brave enough to stand up for yourself and your basic human rights. That part of your person that is above the flaws and fears. This part of you is what brought you to safety in no-man's-land.

Allow Yourself to Feel

When you live from rebellious hope, your feelings no longer need to be bottled up. You can let them go. Feeling the myriad of emotions you need to feel is critical for cleansing your spirit of the negativity and fear your parents forced deep into your psyche and soul. Allow yourself to feel all things. The space of opening, surrendering, and allowing acts as a gateway for your emotions to come to the surface. Your emotions may feel unsafe. However, at your foundation, you are what you feel. Your feelings are the most genuine expression of who you are and the unique ways in which you take the world in. Each emotion has a message of guidance and wisdom. Emotions teach you about who and what is right for you, and who or what is not.

Connect with Your Feelings

The simplest way to connect with your feelings is to ask yourself how you feel, good or bad, in any given moment.

Here is a process that can help you connect with your negative emotions.

- Make a list of negative emotions you experience most frequently, such as afraid, angry, unworthy, confused, sad, terrified, heartbroken, or defeated.

- Write down each emotion on a separate piece of paper and list the situations that trigger this emotion.

- Write down how each emotion feels inside your body (for example, stomachache, nervousness, or trouble breathing).

- Write down the ways this emotion impacts your behavior (for example, being too afraid to take risks, avoiding conflict, or losing your temper).

- Examine how this emotion may, in some strange way, have a loving intention for you. For example, anger may be signaling you when enough is enough. Unworthiness may be telling you that the relationship you are in is not healthy for you. Sadness may be letting you know that you have been hurt. Resentment may be letting you know when you are being taken advantage of.

- Remember that "e-motion" is energy in motion. Ask yourself what actions your feelings are signaling you to take (for example, set a boundary, face a conflict, create distance, or gray-rock).

- Ask yourself who and how you would be if you didn't have these emotions (for example, more confident, fearless, or self-assured).

- Imagine placing your emotion in a basket. See it in there and feel that emotion with all your heart. Thank the emotion for its loving intention toward you. Envision the basket illuminating with light and the emotion turning to vapor, returning you to a state of peace.

Release Hurt Feelings, Grow, and Heal

Hurt feelings simply don't vanish on their own. If you don't release them, they pile up like debt and eventually come due in the most nonproductive ways. Abuse and manipulation erode your resiliency. It is not your fault. It is, however, your responsibility to start rebuilding your capacity for resiliency. The place to start is learning to hold knowledge and mastery over the emotions your parents so cruelly manipulated for their selfish need for power.

In no-man's-land, you learn that being fully human means navigating the gray areas, finding your bottom lines, and embracing the truth of the trauma responsible for your pain. There is no such thing as always agreeing. Your bottom lines will be different than your parents' and many other people's. That doesn't matter. What matters is that you know your bottom lines, what you will and will not tolerate. If there were only agreement, you would not be able to grow as a person.

Every opportunity is one of growth. Show poise, ownership, and tolerance toward yourself in these growing moments. Tolerating abuse from your parents because they are your parents gets you nowhere. This isn't about blaming your parents as much as it's about taking responsibility for yourself. Your parents will always blame you. This keeps them safe from having to look at themselves. What you will find is that your emotionally abusive parents do not reinvent the wheel, they just keep telling the same lies over and again.

Let them go, keep healing, and reinvent your own wheel.

CHAPTER 14

Healing Is a Verb

There is a big difference between *being healed* and *healing.* There is no such thing as being fully healed from the trauma caused by parental abuse and manipulation. Like it or not, you are biologically or adoptively connected to the parents who raised you. The pain you experience at the loss of your parents will always be a part of who you are and who you become. Welcome the idea that you will always be in the process of healing and enhancing your life. Look at *healing* as a verb, an action, and a direction rather than a destination. Healing is an engaging, active process that works on every part of your person. The emotional pain that you experience today will always be filtered through how you learned to deal with pain over the course of your life. There is no way to fully separate yourself psychologically from the people who raised you. The boundaries you set can insulate you only from further abuse.

Healing Is an Inside Job

Outsiders often erroneously assume that if you have separated yourself from your emotionally abusive parents that you are healed, that you are free. In some respects, this is true. You have liberated yourself from being under their authoritarian rule. However, it couldn't be more untrue to assume you don't still have a love for your parents. First, that's not possible. You don't separate yourself or create distance from parents unless the abuse and manipulation weren't destructive enough to do so. No person, regardless of age, wants distance or no contact from the most foundational, important people in their life. If you are in no-man's-land, your parents left you with no other healthy choice. This is something outsiders have trouble conceptualizing because of the perpetuated myths around perfect parents and happy homes woven deeply into the fabric of our culture. There is no room in our cultural narrative that includes a language for bad parents. Remember how we talked about the images of picture-perfect families that result from googling the word "parents." Ads, TV shows, movies, and mass media feature these same images of perfect parents and happy homes. Even when these seemingly ideal parents falter, it is still viewed as well intentioned. There is no abuse that comes from a good intention. Abuse comes from abusive, controlling intentions. This culturally perpetuated myth of perfect parents and happy homes makes healing your wounds more challenging. This myth doesn't consider or protect the real victim, the voiceless child of any age.

For radical healing to occur, I suggest you start using the four A's of healing.

Acknowledgment

Acknowledge and accept that healing hurts and is often a tremendously lonely journey. Acknowledge that the loneliness you feel isn't always about a lack of supportive and loving people in your life, but a lack of people who fully understand what it is to endure having to separate or create distance from your own parents.

Accountability

The healthiest approach to healing is to internally hold your parents accountable for the damage they have caused. Accountability is established through the boundaries you set. Your parents may have created your problems, but they are now your problems to fix. Setting limits on their negative influence on your life and over your person is the correct and healthy choice.

Acceptance

The first step in acceptance is accepting your parents for the abusive people they are. You may always want your parents to be different, but when you can accept them for who they choose to be, you will not need them to be different.

The second step of acceptance is self-acceptance. Embrace that being left no other healthy option but to create distance or set definitive boundaries with your parents is nothing to be ashamed of. You are not a bad person. You are a person who loves yourself enough to protect yourself from further mistreatment.

Action

Healing moves your life in a new and more positive direction. Healing gives you a new story and a sense of possibility. A part of your life will always be back in the pain of your upbringing, but your life—the one you have agency over—is also right here, right now, and you owe it to yourself this very moment to create the best and healthiest life that you can.

This type of active healing leads you through the process of becoming and feeling more whole. It allows you to look in all the crevices where your recovery is needed. The more whole you feel, the more wholeheartedly, bravely, and vibrantly you live. Healing your whole person brings you into harmony with who you are and the value you hold.

"Whole-istic" Healing

I changed the word "holistic" to "whole-istic" for a special reason, and that reason is you. *Holistic* healing implies natural, effortless, or organic. For most survivors of parental emotional abuse, there is nothing natural, effortless, or organic about having to create distance from or cut off your parents, let alone push against the heavily indoctrinated myth that all parents are good and love their children. Further, there is nothing natural in parents manipulating and abusing the children they raise. Whether emotional, sexual, verbal, or physical, violence is the lowest form of communication. You deserve so much more than the lowest form of anything. For these reasons, I created a new version of *whole-istic* for you to strive for.

The desire to feel whole is fundamental to the human spirit. You desire to feel safe and secure not just with others, but most importantly within yourself. Wholeness, which you gain through self-actualization, is the process by which you realize your fullest potential. Having been raised by abusive and manipulative parents, you left childhood far from whole. You left with holes. These holes act like open wounds. The more conscious you are of your holes, what and where they are, how they developed, and what they mean to you and for you, the better you become in protecting and healing those holes.

Following is a guided path toward creating inner wholeness. This process will require you to focus healing energy on yourself on every level, including physical, emotional, mental, financial, relational, and spiritual.

Physical Healing

There is a field of study called *psychoneuroimmunology*, which explains how thoughts and feelings impact physical well-being. Many years ago, I came across a book called *Heal Your Body* by Louise Hay (Hay 1984). In this book, Hay connects physical ailments to psychological counterparts. The physical level of the human being acts as a person's foundation. Everything else is built upon that. This means that if you're not physically well, it will prove difficult to be emotionally, mentally, financially, relationally, or spiritually well. As an example of how physical healing works, following are physical ailments that Hay lists in her book that I have experienced with some consistency over the course of my life, along with corresponding psychological explanations.

- **Accident prone:** inability to speak up for myself, defiant against authority

- **Aches:** yearning for love

- **Adrenal problems:** family tension, child feeling unwelcome and in the way, exhaustion, nervousness

- **Anorexia:** rejecting the self and life, extreme fear, self-hate

- **Anxiety:** not trusting the process, need for control

- **Asthma:** smothered by love, inability to breathe for myself, feeling suffocated

- **Bronchitis:** inflamed family environments

- **Cough:** desire to shout at the world, "See me, listen to me"

- **Depression:** anger, guilt for feeling hopeless

- **Headaches:** self-criticism, fear

- **High cholesterol:** blocking the channels of enjoyment, fear of embracing joy

- **Hip pain:** clumps of stubborn anger at parents, nothing to move forward to

- **Hyperactivity:** fear, feeling pressured and frantic

- **Insomnia:** fear, anxiety

- **Laryngitis:** so angry I can't speak, scared to speak up, resentment of authority

- **Loss of appetite:** fear, not trusting life

- **Low blood pressure:** lack of love as a child, anguish

- **Mono:** anger at not receiving love and appreciation, not caring for myself

- **Motion sickness:** fear, especially of not being in control

- **Postnasal drip:** inner crying, inner-child tears

- **Sore throat:** holding in angry words, feeling unable to express feelings, fear of conflict

- **Upper-back pain:** lack of emotional support, feeling unloved, holding feelings in

In Hay's book, each ailment comes with an affirmation to repeat to yourself to help heal your mind and body. Instead of using the affirmations given in the book, I made up my own to personalize my healing and suggest you do the same. For example, for my asthma the healing affirmation I repeat is: "I am thankful I now breathe deeply, easily, and effortlessly on my own, knowing my healthy boundaries are in place. I am safe and protected from the parents who harmed me."

When your physical body is healthy, your moods and reactions are easier to manage. When your thoughts and emotions are more manageable, you are more in touch with the essence of your resilient and beautiful spirit and better understand the purpose of your life, love, and relationships.

Emotional Healing

To heal emotionally takes a deep, naked honesty. A critical pillar of emotional healing is learning to harness your emotions before acting them out. It is imperative to train yourself to slow down and taste the words you speak before spitting them out. Otherwise, you can end up emotionally damaging yourself and others in the same ways your parents damaged you. Having a history of trauma can make managing defensiveness, neediness, and control feel nearly impossible. Learning to be with what you feel, rather than to impulsively act upon how you feel, helps you gather the all-important quality of discernment. *Discernment* means to possess good judgment. It makes sense, then, that to be discerning, self-control would be a critical aspect of the development of your emotional intelligence. To heal in this area, let's examine the mechanics of your emotions.

Emotions move through your central nervous system, which includes your spinal cord and brain. Different parts of your brain process emotions differently. Once emotions enter the base of your brain, they move to your limbic system in the midbrain. It is in the limbic system where you become aware of an emotion and give it a label (such as some variation of mad, sad, glad, afraid, ashamed, or hurt). Once an emotion is labeled, there is an automatic reaction or associated behavior linked to that emotion. This is when you're most vulnerable to speaking or acting before reasoning. When you act without thinking, you are in "limbic overload." When you are in limbic overload, you are overemoting and under-reasoning. To counter a knee-jerk response to an emotion and exercise self-control, try to pause before reacting. This gives your emotions time to move from your limbic system into the frontal part of your brain, where executive functioning, such as reasoning, emotional regulation, and judgment, takes place. Once this happens, you're better able to decide how you want to respond to the emotion you're feeling.

Mental Healing

The prefrontal cortex is the part of the brain that houses rational thought, allowing you to reason through what you feel, why you feel it, and what you would like the bigger-picture outcome to be when deciding to communicate your emotions to others. Your ability to apply logic can help improve your mental health. The prefrontal cortex tempers your actions until you have established emotional regulation, guaranteeing the solidity of what is true for you to come forth. This enables you to set boundaries and communicate clearly. When you have your emotional mind and mental mind working well together, you improve your ability to make good decisions. When you can count on yourself to make good decisions, it helps you trust yourself to make the right decisions.

One of the most effective ways to get your emotions under control is to write them out in a journal, which requires the involvement of your prefrontal cortex. Here are some benefits of journaling what you feel. Journaling helps you:

- prioritize your problems, fears, worries, and stressors

- avoid emotional outbursts (impulsivity), improving your psychological insight and therefore mood

- get clear on who you are and what your feelings need to find a place of resolve

- track day-to-day moods or patterns that prove helpful in recognizing triggers and developing strategies to better manage them

- develop positive self-talk and identify nonproductive thoughts and behaviors

- craft and maintain a sense of self and solidify your identity

- reflect on your experiences and discover your authentic self

- possess the beautiful quality of discernment

Financial Healing

You may be wondering why I am including money as a place of healing in your wholeness. Money is a tool, but it is also emotionally loaded. For this reason, read all you can about the spirit of money—how to attract it, respect it, and appreciate it. Work to become as financially independent as possible to eliminate your emotionally abusive parents' coercive control over your financial life and independence. You deserve the riches life has to offer, especially when your hard work brings rewards of abundance. The more balanced you are with money, the less debt you have, the less stressed, more in control, and closer to whole you feel. Further, money, when well managed, can provide a sense of predictability, consistency, and security that you didn't get from your parents. Money may not bring happiness, but it does bring freedom. Having enough money to remove finance as a major stress in your life, or at least reduce any negative emotional impact it has, helps enable you to captain your own ship. Having this type of agency over your life is fundamental to wholeness.

Relational Healing

When you have yourself together as a working unit physically, emotionally, mentally, and financially, you enter relationships with a greater sense of mastery over your life. It is never too late to undertake this process of evolvement. One gift of wholeness is that it takes the responsibility off others to heal your childhood wounds. When you take this approach, you are less controlling, afraid, needy, defensive, and unhappy in your relationships. It feels good to be responsible for your own life. In no-man's-land, you come to understand that responsibility and mental health go together. When you are whole, you are more likely to attract that wholeness back to you in the relationships you choose to keep.

> **Moment of truth:** In healthy relationships, things are clear, not confusing.

Markers of a healthy relationship include the following.

- You feel free to engage in deep and meaningful conversations.

- You feel safe to share your vulnerabilities.

- You feel safe to show up as who you are in your varying moods.

- You feel seen and understood.

- You feel accepted.

- You feel encouraged and supported to grow.

- Your independence is celebrated.

- You are comfortable with your flaws.

- You can be playful and lighthearted.

- You feel at ease with silence and personal space, and with the space others need.

- You value nonsexual and sexual intimacy.

- You hold yourself and others accountable.

- You create the space to express your emotions freely through both your highs and your lows.

- You have a deep respect for yourself and others.

These relationship markers are what ignite your spirit and reopen your heart to love and belonging—two things that caused you to suffer the deepest as a child because you lacked them. Being open to love and able to love without defensively blocking your authenticity is liberating. It's a wonderful experience to feel connected to those you love from your whole self. When love is present, life has significance and meaning, as does what you have suffered. The healthier you become, the healthier your relationships become.

Spiritual Healing

Spirituality implies connection. Your connection could be to self, the Universe, God, or others, for example, and to the overall process of life. Choosing to heal yourself is the most self-actualizing process to undertake. Through this process, you can savor truly knowing that something magical has been loving, supporting, and protecting you up to this point and will continue to look out for you.

Being spiritual involves being flexible to go in the directions that life leads you. As a spiritual being, you are always in motion. Change is a constant. The more spiritual you grow to be, the more you realize how ineffective clutching and hanging on to toxic relationships has been and what it has cost you. Flow is the secret ingredient to seeing your trauma through spiritual eyes. You must be willing to bend and flex with the changing tides of your healing journey. Seeing your trauma through existential eyes can help you take in the bigger-picture lessons. When you can live from this mindset, it helps you focus on who and what you have, rather than on who or what you have lost. There is always a silver-lining possibility when you embrace the more spiritual perceptions and ideals of life. You can see the warrior spirit you embody and the growth opportunities you created out of your most terrorizing moments. This is a superpower.

CHAPTER 15

Your Happiness Possibility

Wholeness leads to happiness, which means happiness is a real possibility for you. You deserve to be happy. It is not selfish, and you are not betraying anyone in choosing to live your best life. Blinded by the cultural myths of perfect parents and happy homes, many people will never understand the painful path you have traveled. You will face that kickback for the rest of your life. Accept it. You don't owe anyone an explanation for protecting yourself. Your decision speaks for itself. Being understood is overrated. Seeking to be understood in this situation is re-wounding at best. In no-man's-land, it becomes clear that you do not need to waste your existence seeking to be understood. There is no power in that existence. You will not find yourself in other people's approval. The power you have inside you is far more stable. Understand, love, and accept yourself. This is the key to your happiness possibility.

Taking charge of your life does not need to be a loud or boastful production where you are posturing with your defenses to show your parents that you are doing fine without them. Live elegantly and quietly. Live in your peace. You know that you did not ask to be abused. You also know you were strong enough to stop your abuse. Taking the abuse was horrible, and getting away from the abuse was equally, if not even more, painful. Let it be. The path of a GOAT is not designed to be easy. The survivor's way is your spirituality. You may travel alone for a while and feel lonely on your evolvement path.

In no-man's-land, you feel the depths of being alone in your journey, rejected by both family and society. *Aloneness* is having no one else present, whereas *loneliness* is being without love. You have always been lonely in your toxic family. It didn't matter how many people were around. There was no love. One of the hardest things to adapt to in no-man's-land is being alone. It is a double whammy when you feel aloneness and loneliness in no-man's-land.

It's all part of the journey. You often find your way into your wholeness solitarily.

Turn Insecurities into Superpowers

I understand and respect that opening your heart is not easy after all you have endured. It is also challenging to digest that your parents needed you to feel insecure to keep you under their control. Toxic parents cannot tolerate being challenged. To keep you feeling small and isolated, they systematically programmed you to view life through a lens of darkness, their darkness. Toxic parents weren't looking for children, they were looking for emotional prisoners—people they could control. What they failed to consider is that one day you would become so fed up that you would amputate them from your life, just to feel a sense of relief. This oversight was their critical mistake. Amputating the most influential people from your life may not have been accomplished from a place of security, but it certainly came from somewhere inside of you. You reached a point where enough was enough, and insecurity became the driving force to set you free.

I have found that my deepest insecurities have also been my most profound visionaries and greatest saviors that have helped me heal. In a twisted irony, your insecurities are the North Star that have the power to lead you to happiness. Survivors come by insecurities honestly. They are the holes in your heart that make you human. They make you real. They give your existence meaning and direction. They are the road map leading down the path of self-discovery. What I realized in no-man's-land is that I, and many of you, misunderstand our insecurities. You likely do all you can to split them off from your identity by overcompensating for them. The lack of understanding of the purpose of your insecurities can contribute to your ending up in damaging relationships as an adult. It doesn't need to be this way. Insecurities are not bad, and they don't make you annoying or repulsive unless you choose to keep them in the shadows—unseen, untamed, and unmanaged. It is critical you bring your insecurities out of the dark and assimilate them into your personality.

Here are some ways to see the value in your insecurities.

Make a List of Your Insecurities

Write down the things you imagine the people you wish to impress are saying about you behind your back. Writing your insecurities down shrinks them from a looming, cloudy embellished anxiety in your head and puts them into words on paper that can be dissected and discussed. Next, whisper this list out loud to give your fears form in the shape of audible words. Spelling out your insecurities and hearing them audibly helps release their death grip over you that can cause you to overcompensate.

Share Your Insecurities with a Trusted Friend or Therapist

Verbalizing your imperfections decreases their power. Insecurities thrive in the shadows. When you shine a light on them and expose them to trusted others, you begin to understand and overcome them. The power of vulnerability is that it makes you human. There is a precious connectedness you forge with others because the demons you face are never yours alone. Owning and sharing them means they cannot be used by others to wound you.

Find the Humor

Humor is powerful enough to evict shame. When you allow yourself to laugh at the cuteness and humanity of your flaws and foibles, the more playful you have the potential to become, and the more comfortable other people feel to express or own their own flaws and foibles when in your presence.

Use Insecurities as Signposts

Your insecurities, when used correctly, can be signposts leading you directly to your inner wounding. Knowing your wounds allows you to heal them.

See the Opportunity

Look at your insecurities as spiritual assignments. Consider how your insecurities can give you a fresh and new perspective to help guide you toward its opposite. Ask each insecurity what its opportunity for growth is.

Recognize What Insecurity Tells You About Others

When you risk sharing your open, raw, exposed self with another person, that person's treatment of you will tell you everything you need to know about them and whether they will or will not fit into your life. This is gold.

Embrace Your Insecurities

Insecurity isn't about pretending to feel differently than you do. There is no point in that. Yet so many of you do all you can to overcompensate for your imperfections, including concealing them, ignoring them, or dancing around them and pretending they don't have a hold over you. Every person has insecurities, so take a deep breath. Put the 10,000-pound gorilla down and let it be. You're okay. Your woundedness deserves compassion and you as a trusted companion.

Surviving parental emotional abuse has likely turned you into one of the most skilled people you know when it comes to reading the behaviors and emotions of others. Because you had to survive abuse, you cannot help but be hyperattuned to minor shifts in body language and other nuances in behavior, often making you the first to notice when someone is a bit off.

These are beautiful and life-saving gifts to come from your insecurities. When tapped, insecurities can lead you to increased wisdom. For example, my insecurities have led me to be a better partner, friend, therapist, and writer. So many of my favorite qualities have arisen from my insecurities. My deep empathy, humility, and capacity to sit with pain and discomfort come from my insecurities. My capacity to understand and relate to the raw humanity in others comes through my insecurities. When you can bring your imperfections out of the shadow of shame, you meet yourself and others in a space of tenderness. This a beautiful thing. Stop berating yourself for having insecurities. Instead, allow them to bless you.

You Must Choose Happiness to Find Happiness

As a survivor, you may often experience a relief from stress as happiness. Relief is not happiness. Relief is a feeling of closure or reassurance, or an emotional break following some type of a reprieve from unbearable feelings, such as anxiety and distress. Happiness, on the other hand, is simply the state of being happy. You were raised by parents who made you feel happiness was too big of an ask, so you settled for relief. You must ask what the point would be of having survived all these steps if not to embrace the happiness possibility you sacrificed everything to have. It's hard to conceptualize happiness when the only thing you have ever sought has been relief.

If you have made it this far, you may as well keep going to strive to live not just for moments of relief but also for a lifetime of real happiness. It is your right to be the happiest person you have the potential to be. To do this, you must make the conscious choice to practice happiness until it becomes your new state of being. Here are some ways to do that.

- **Be Purposeful** Live with intention. Live your life on purpose. Become a great manager of your life and person through intentional actions, such as making lists, having goals, following through, and choosing good company.

- **Accept Rejection** Rejection is a necessary part of life. Remember, each no takes you one step closer to a yes. To each no, learn to say next.

- **Make Life Fun** Do life in a way that makes you smile. You deserve it.

- **Take Risks** Ultimately, everything you dream of is on the other side of your fear. You can do it. All you must do now is start.

- **Dream About Your Future** Imagine the life you want, put images that represent your wishes on a vision board, and manifest all that you desire.

- **Make Today Better** Each morning that you wake up, ask yourself how you can make this particular day a great day. Allowing each day to be a day of greater improvement and a day of even deeper reflection leads to increased freedom to be yourself.

- **Let the Past Guide You** Rearview mirrors help you take experiences that are behind you and use them to guide you with wisdom each day. Allow yesterday's pain to introduce you to today's joy.

- **Embrace Love** Love is fundamental to happiness, confidence, and your mental and emotional well-being.

Choose Good Company

A critical element of maximizing your happiness possibility is choosing good company. I have come to wholeheartedly believe that emotional abuse survivors are capable of intimacy in ways that people who didn't have as tragic a childhood are not. I look at survivors and know that you are some of the healthiest people out there. What wasn't healthy was your background. For instance, I have treated and known many people who have had far healthier upbringings than my own and your own, and they aren't nearly as mentally or emotionally mature or insightful. Their emotional intelligence isn't as high because they haven't had to walk through the types of emotional pain you have had to for them to know how to navigate pain when it pops up. This lack of emotional intelligence and experience can make them incredibly insensitive, dismissive, and short-sighted toward the pain of others.

Be grateful that you know how to use your insecurity to better your life. You have seen and experienced things those who have lived a more sheltered life have not, so your possibility for happiness and expansion also surpasses that of many others. You have had to go to the deepest parts of yourself to find yourself, and this is beautiful. You are the person you must live with every day, and you have made sure that you are good company for you. For more good company, pick people to be in your life who uplift you.

Navigate Gaps in Understanding

The differences in emotional intelligence discussed above are what create gaps in understanding between ourselves and the partners and friends we pull into our lives. For a survivor, this gap can feel painful and dismissive when someone is trying to be helpful but unknowingly gives you ignorant and offensive advice or feedback. For example, if we are opening up about the abuse we sustained by a parent, a person who doesn't understand this might say, "Well, you are loved by so many, and that parent is only one person." A parent is far deeper and more critically significant than just any one person. Because the new people in your life may have no concept of the depths of emotional abuse, they often mistakenly say the wrong things when trying to help. In these situations, be patient. Patience will give the people on the other side of you time to grow.

You don't have to choose to love people who have your same or similar trauma in order to be understood. What you need is people who are capable of loving and respecting you. If they cannot empathize with your circumstances but can sympathize, allow that to be enough. If someone has not lived the experience of emotionally abusive and manipulative parents, they will not be able to fully get it. That is okay.

It is not uncommon when you are first in new relationships that these people have the desire to fix the relationship between you and your parents. This can feel deeply minimizing of the fact that you have already done all the heart-wrenching, terrifying work to create the necessary distance. There is nothing to be fixed when the distance you have created has already done the job. Directly, but gently, be clear with the person who wants to fix things that are already fixed, according to what your needs are and the fact that there is no going back. Many erroneously believe that fixing means reconciliation, when in your case it means decreased or no contact. You must allow time and conversation to help those who love you come to accept that you know what is best for you. Fortunately, your toxic parents will reveal their abusive ways in due time to everyone who loves you. Ironically, your parents could be the people whose actions establish common ground between you and those who love you.

Be mindful of not using new relationships as an avenue to heal the wounds left by your parents and other involved family. Throughout your healing, it will remain your life's work to dig deep to continue your commitment to healing your own wounds. Relationships will bring out your insecurities. It's okay. This is what brings love in.

Here are some signposts that you are in a healthy relationship.

- You feel emotionally safe, content, and peaceful after spending time together.

- You can be your whole self around them.

- They are on your team.

- They do not put you down or hold you back.

- You can let your guard down.

- They bring you peace rather than problems.

- They are consistent in their lovingness through both highs and lows.

- They lift you up and believe in you, even when you don't believe as fully in yourself.

- They make you happy.

CHAPTER 16

Make Love Your Default Emotion

There are two core emotions—love and fear. Other emotions sprout from those two. Love is the one emotion every human being wants. At your core, you are the essence of love. You are not fear. Anger comes from fear. Happiness and excitement come from love. Control comes from fear. Vulnerability comes from love. Being raised in fear blocks your experience of love. How you feel is critical to how you live and experience all of life. If you feel fear, you will live from fear. If you feel love, you will live from love. It's time to start living your new life and to exit no-man's-land.

You Are Lovable

Know that you are lovable.

Without the love of your parents, you suffered. You suffered deeply. You deserved love from the parents who chose to raise you. You deserved to be loved for exactly who you are. This type of love is effortless to give and receive for parents when they're psychologically healthy. Unconditional love never runs out and is something that makes the connection between a child and their parents supportive, equitable, and balanced. If you were given anything less, it was not love. Manipulation disguised as love will exhaust you.

As a child, you began to ask why it was so impossible for your parents to love you. You reasoned: If my own parents can't love me, I must not be lovable. This is how and when fear took over. Love would never make you feel the ways your parents' "love" made you feel. Abusive and manipulative parents are not a safe place to put your love.

Self-love is a sacred practice that helps you remember who you are. The more you practice, the more inward and outward momentum you create to leave no-man's-land. Here are some ways to create a supply of self-love.

- Move your body at least once each day in a way that makes you feel healthy and alive.
- Make time for peaceful moments.
- Make a conscious effort to take care of your personal space.
- Make time for self-reflection.
- Catch up with a friend.
- Take a social media detox for twenty-four hours.
- Light an aromatic candle.
- Take a bath or enjoy a sauna.
- Create a gratitude list.
- Spend time outdoors.
- Eat life-giving, soul-enriching foods.
- Spend time with those who love you.
- Read a fiction book.
- Try something new.
- Go away for a weekend.
- Watch a movie.
- Listen to music.
- Make a vision board.
- Have lazy days to do nothing.

Self-love comes down to simple habits. It manifests itself in parts of your life, such as:

- how you spend your time

- how you talk to yourself

- what you read

- what you watch

- whom you share your energy with

- whom you allow to have access to you

Moment of truth: It is possible to love yourself in all the ways your parents didn't. It is possible to accept yourself in all the ways you were never accepted.

When you have those days where it feels impossible to love yourself, you have simply fallen out of alignment with your power. Do not try and force the love back in. Acknowledge that you're having a moment of being out of alignment. Feel what you need to feel and deal with the discomfort so you can heal this sad and lost moment. It is just a moment. Sometimes, loving yourself means allowing bad days, sad moods, and lonely moments. That's life. That is part of what it means to be whole. Let it come, let it go, and reset back to love.

Remindful exercises have the power to shift your energy immediately. When you feel down, for example, it can be helpful to make a list of good, basic things in life you are worthy of. Here are some reminders to get you started. You are worthy of the following:

- love

- trust

- feeling safe

- joy, elation, excitement, success, and happiness
- being treated with love and respect
- being and feeling heard
- freedom to be yourself
- tolerance when you don't get it right
- compromise
- being approached for an explanation rather than with accusation
- another's willingness to talk about the hard stuff
- encouragement
- love and adoration each day
- compliments
- equality
- peace
- respect
- follow-through

Identifying what you are worthy of is an important aspect of loving, knowing, and honoring yourself. You deserved parents who offered you all of these, but all is not lost when this was not your reality. The love you can never lose is the love you learn to have in yourself and for yourself.

Love Yourself as If You Were Your Own Child

To successfully make love your new default emotion, start investing in the details of who you are. Getting to know yourself is and will continue to be an enlightening journey as you design an inner map of your person. Depending on your interests, this can happen in many different ways, including reading books, learning about your astrological chart, investigating numerology, knowing your Myers-Briggs personality type, seeing your Human Design chart, exploring the Enneagram, and understanding your physical health and what different illnesses in your body reflect about your psychological state. Look high, low, and everywhere in between in your discovery process. Inviting this type of self-discovery into your life allows you to separate yourself as fundamentally different from the false narrative told of you. I guarantee, as the truth and depth of your story unfolds within, you will discover you're quite amazing. Theses aha moments will have you shining more radiantly. You are a person who was raised in poison but somehow kept the purity of your inner whispers alive. You, my friend, are someone to be proud of. The most valiant thing you can do is heal yourself, so other people do not have to heal from you.

Three Aspects of Self

Throughout my journey as a survivor, what I have craved more than anything was getting to know who I really was underneath all the negative and fear-based conditioning. I no longer wanted to see myself as small, dejected, and invisible. Because healing is an ongoing process, there are still days where I, and you, will fall into these painful feeling states. However, as I continue to evolve, I have come up with a healing paradigm I have found to be incredibly useful in getting myself and others through those painful times. I call this healing paradigm the three *aspects of self*, which include the child self, present-day self, and future self. Each person is made up of three different coexisting parts, with all three parts being in motion and all impacting the other. Using myself as the example:

- The first aspect of me is the Sherrie behind me ("Little Sherrie"). She is my past.

- The second aspect is the Sherrie I am today ("Present-Day Sherrie"). She is my present.

- The third aspect is the Sherrie in my future who I am in the process of becoming ("Future Sherrie"). She is my goal and my greatest desire.

My Child Self

Little Sherrie starts from yesterday and goes back to my birth. She offers rearview mirror guidance and is the keeper of my pain. When understood correctly, she proves to be an incredible guide to the other two aspects of me. Little Sherrie is a vault. She is the child who holds the history, tragedies, hurts, core wounds, sensitivities, important memories, and defining moments of both pain and triumph. She is the part of me that holds the delicate, vulnerable, loud, scared, frenetic feelings and painful memories. Little Sherrie struggles to trust and is terrified of abandonment. She is the aspect of me that has been conditioned to believe she is fatally flawed and unlovable. She has had to endure the most disgusting abuses at the hands of her parents and other involved family and friends all by herself. This aspect of me is the most in need of my attention, nurturing, patience, and unconditional love. She is also the piece of me that helps me recognize when I am repeating patterns of old trauma as Present-Day Sherrie.

My Present-Day Self

In no-man's-land, I learned that when I allowed Little Sherrie to keep my focus transfixed on the traumas in the rearview mirror, I found myself involved in one life collision after another. She is the part of me that Present-Day Sherrie has been the most hateful, cruel, and insensitive to, just as my parents taught me to be. Present-Day Sherrie learned to speak a language of loathing to Little Sherrie's needs and fears. Present-Day Sherrie needed Little Sherrie to silence her voice, so she wouldn't expose my vulnerabilities and repulsive qualities to the larger world. I learned to hate her for being needy, for needing me, for needing my parents, for needing anyone at all. Little Sherrie was always whispering to me, and it annoyed me because needing people had proven to be debilitating to the person I am today. I hated Little Sherrie. I hated her low self-esteem. She always wanted validation, didn't perform up to standard, wasn't pretty or thin enough, wasn't smart, was too weak to stand up for herself, lived her life barely making it, and was ultimately not a person anyone would like because she was too pathetic, feeble, and desperate. She tried way too hard, and it was beyond annoying.

For many years, I abandoned Little Sherrie, just as my parents did. I believed that it was Little Sherrie's fault that my parents didn't love me, so I felt she deserved my abandonment. Because Present-Day Sherrie didn't take care of Little Sherrie, she wreaked havoc in my life. I was consistently entering relationships of all kinds in which people manipulated and abused me in the same ways my parents did. These replicating experiences made Little Sherrie grow in power but, unbeknownst to me, also in her truth. I had spent most of my life feeling totally useless when trying to get this child-self aspect of me to mature, so I could find some sense of peace. She was too big for Present-Day Sherrie to control.

At this point in my healing, I didn't have any concept that there was a more mature, confident, elegant version of me to call on, until one day while journaling, this three-part paradigm revealed itself. It has been life-changing. I am happy to say that Present-Day Sherrie has changed a lot. I choose to learn from Little Sherrie's wisdom. I allow her to teach me. When she is hurt, I nurture and listen to her. I give her the compassion and understanding I never received from my parents. I realize and respect that Little Sherrie has always held the truth. She has never lied to me. I refused to listen to her, just as I was never listened to when I was her. I hear her now.

Of all the parts of me, I have come to learn that Little Sherrie is the real hero. She survived all the abuse and degradation, and she survived it all by herself. She was brave enough to persist in telling me her truths until I finally listened. She pestered Present-Day Sherrie to wake me up. Today,

I admire her persistence. She's the child in me who deserves a good parent, and I can do this for her myself. So can you.

My Future Self

I got comfortable and happy in the relationship between my past and my present selves in no-man's-land. After reading *The Alchemist* by Paulo Coelho (1993) and *Women Who Run with the Wolves* by Clarissa Pinkola Estés (1989), I started daydreaming about the idea of Future Sherrie—the woman I have always been yearning to become. I explored who I sensed she was by writing down her imagined characteristics in my journal. I started falling in love with her and practicing her character traits (as you just learned to do). She is discerning, self-assured, quiet, truthful, successful, loving to self and others, and careful with her time and the people she chooses to spend it with. She is a woman of her word, keeps the company of a small group of friends, treasures alone time, is wise, invests in growing, speaks only the truth, and is a goddess. She is spiritual, accepting, peaceful, helpful, compassionate, intelligent, poised, disciplined, playful, funny, accepting, feminine, vibrant, abundant, firm, worthy, admired, adored, audacious, fun-loving, lighthearted, deep, calm, open, vulnerable, imperfect, private, emotionally available, outdoorsy, present, and graceful. As I listed out these characteristics, I made a vision board to start the process of becoming her. I feel deeply compelled toward becoming her each day. My soul is her soul, and she's leading me down the path of my highest evolvement, providing me a model of the woman I strive to be. Becoming Future Sherrie continues to be the greatest and most passionate pursuit of my life.

I call on my future self to guide who I am today. When I feel triggered by Little Sherrie's insecurities, I no longer, as Present-Day Sherrie, push Little Sherrie away. I do not criticize, berate, or abandon her. I call on Future Sherrie for her imagined wisdom to guide and help me nurture, be present to, and genuinely love the forever more vulnerable, reactive, exposed, life-fearing Little Sherrie. When I am being challenged, I look to

Future Sherrie to digest fears that are haunting me from Little Sherrie. I allow the three parts of who I am to engage in a meaningful conversation, collaborating, healing, and being the wholeness of who I am. I no longer engage in the inner habit of separation and division against myself, as I had learned to do from the divide-and-conquer environment my parents raised me in. I do not abuse myself. I have well overpaid my emotional dues in that arena of life. The language I speak over each aspect of myself is one of love, compassion, and acceptance. This is my wish for all of you, for you to love, embrace, and accept all of who you are.

> **Moment of truth:** To know love is to know yourself.

This "know thyself" discovery process will have you holding a deeper concern about yourself than ever before. You will care about your overall health and well-being and shift your nonfunctional habits to more functional ones, not because you must, but because you care about yourself enough to do so. You are in a relationship with yourself, a human being you both love and admire. This is the whole purpose of life. It can be painful, dark, arduous, confusing, scary, liberating, sensational, growth-promoting, horrifying, exhilarating, and freeing. Healing is the hero's journey because cycles of family emotional abuse end only if you break them. You are this person.

Lean into Love

Love is the most powerful force in the Universe. It is the only life-force energy common to all living things, including the planets, stars, and galaxies. Love is the energetic current that connects people to themselves and to each other. It is the frequency of love that created you, not your emotionally abusive parents. The greatest miracle parents can bring into their life is a child. When you have been treated as the greatest burden of their life, it is nearly impossible to believe miracles exist, let alone that you are the miracle of life you were born to be. Your toxic parents have never connected to you on the frequency of love. For whatever reason, they do not choose the miracle of love. They are, instead, seduced by pride. That is no longer your problem. That is the choice your parents made and not a choice you are willing to make. When you release yourself from the darkness where their prideful ways drain your spirit, miracles will begin to uplift your life.

I am here to tell you that miracles do exist and you—yes, you—are a miracle or you would not be here, reading this book and working on changing your life. It makes logical sense that if by your nature, your DNA, you are a miracle, then you must also be worthy of miracles and the belief that you can manifest them. Once you shift from pain being your purpose to love being your purpose, life changes. I have come to believe that survivors like you and me have always been divinely guided. There is no other explanation for how we got to this place in our lives if something hadn't been looking over us. It certainly wasn't our parents, so it must have been the vibration of love. This vibration of love has given me a voice to speak about my experience as a wounded healer. As a wounded healer, I have chosen to turn my perpetrators into my purpose—to make it out of the hell I was raised in and through no-man's-land. I have and will continue to create a life that somehow makes sense. If I can do it, so can you.

You Are the Miracle

The kind of work you are doing to heal yourself is nothing short of major surgery. To heal your core and challenge a society that perpetuates a myth of perfect parents and happy homes is beyond brave. It is heroic. In changing yourself, you are also changing the lives of others by helping to normalize that abusive and manipulative parents are real and destroy the mental health and well-being of their children. To live your happiness possibility, you must become your own advocate, lobbyist, and supporter. You can do this! You can become the miracle of love you have always been looking for.

Healing is truly miraculous when you have come from a loveless beginning. Life has been so hard. Then, one day, you start seeing the fruits of your labor. You start waking up in this place where things make sense. Your heart is at peace. You have accepted your circumstances and learned to move with your pain. Freedom from pain allows your soul to be unencumbered and radiate light. Your thoughts are finally hopeful in the healthiest of ways because your vision is clear. You hold a genuine respect and admiration for what you've been through and feel at peace with where and how you have been healing.

An exceptionally wonderful moment in any survivor's life is when you realize you can do whatever you want. You no longer owe anyone an explanation for your personal choices and preferences. You don't need anyone's permission. You are out of no-man's-land just living life, and it's beautiful. You recognize and honor that you would not be the person you are right here, right now had you been born under different circumstances. You recognize that having been left to yourself for long enough inspired you to find yourself because there was nothing else for you to look for. You found yourself through all the pain. You picked yourself up time and again, and you kept going. You kept going because of love and your own belief in yourself. The most amazing piece of this is you did find love. You found it in yourself. You capitalized on it and with great wisdom applied it to all of life's ups and downs, knowing that the love you found inside of you has always and will always get you through to the other side.

This is something to be grateful for.

I am so proud of you.

Moment of truth: If you want to see a miracle, look in the mirror.

Acknowledgments

Thank you to my "Framily" for your love and support, to my bravehearted community, and to my team at New Harbinger Publications.

References

Angelou, M. 2006. Interview by D. Chappelle. *Iconoclasts* (Season 2, Episode 6), RadicalMedia, November 30.

Campbell, S. 2022. *Adult Survivors of Toxic Family Members: Tools to Maintain Boundaries, Deal with Criticism, and Heal from Shame After Ties Have Been Cut.* Oakland, CA: New Harbinger Publications.

Coelho, P. 1993. *The Alchemist.* San Francisco: HarperOne.

Hay, L. 1984. *Heal Your Body.* 4th ed. New York: Hay House.

Pinkola Estés, C. 1989. *Women Who Run with the Wolves: Myths and Stories of the Wild Woman Archetype.* New York: Ballentine Books.

Walker, P. 2013. *Complex PTSD: From Surviving to Thriving: A Guide and Map for Recovering from Childhood Trauma.* Scotts Valley, CA: CreateSpace.

Real change *is* possible

For more than forty-five years, New Harbinger has published proven-effective self-help books and pioneering workbooks to help readers of all ages and backgrounds improve mental health and well-being, and achieve lasting personal growth. In addition, our spirituality books offer profound guidance for deepening awareness and cultivating healing, self-discovery, and fulfillment.

Founded by psychologist Matthew McKay and Patrick Fanning, New Harbinger is proud to be an independent, employee-owned company. Our books reflect our core values of integrity, innovation, commitment, sustainability, compassion, and trust. Written by leaders in the field and recommended by therapists worldwide, New Harbinger books are practical, accessible, and provide real tools for real change.

newharbingerpublications

Sherrie Campbell, PhD, is a licensed psychologist who specializes in helping healthy people cut ties with the toxic people in their lives. She is a nationally recognized expert on family estrangement, an inspirational speaker, a social media influencer, and a regularly featured media expert. She is host of the podcast, *Sherapy Sessions*, and author of *Adult Survivors of Toxic Family Members.*

Also by Sherrie Campbell, PhD

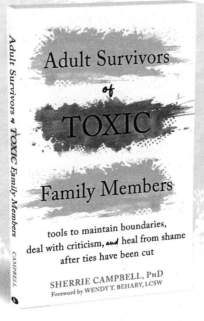

This compassionate guide will help you accept and embrace
your decision to cut ties with a toxic family member; and
provides powerful tools for creating boundaries, coping with
judgment, and overcoming self-doubt.

978-1684039289 / US $17.95

 new**harbinger**publications
1-800-748-6273 / newharbinger.com